Timeless Roots

Timeless Echoes, Volume 2

Angeline Gallant

Published by Crest & Quill Press, 2024.

While every precaution has been taken in the preparation of this book, the publisher assumes no responsibility for errors or omissions, or for damages resulting from the use of the information contained herein.

TIMELESS ROOTS

First edition. December 19, 2024.

Copyright © 2024 Angeline Gallant.

ISBN: 979-8230392767

Written by Angeline Gallant.

Table of Contents

ARSELIA SHANNON

———

ARSELIA SHANNON[1]

In 1855, life was shaped by significant historical, social, and technological contexts, depending on Arselia Shannon's location. Here's an overview of what life might have been like:

Global Context

Industrial Revolution: Technological innovations were transforming economies. Railroads and steamships expanded trade and travel, reducing distances between communities.

Communication Advances: The electric telegraph was widely in use, revolutionizing how information traveled.

Political Shifts: Globally, debates around democracy, nationalism, and colonial expansion were intensifying.

———

NORTH AMERICA (CANADA and the U.S.)

Canada West (Ontario): This was still part of the Province of Canada. Settlers worked hard to establish farms and communities. Railroads like the Grand Trunk Railway were beginning to shape the economic landscape.

Indigenous Displacement: Colonial policies were pushing Indigenous peoples off their lands to make way for settlers.

Slavery and Abolition: Slavery had been abolished in British territories for over 20 years, and Canada was a haven for escaped enslaved people via the Underground Railroad.

DAILY LIFE

Rural Living: Most people lived on farms, relying on manual labor for agriculture. Life revolved around family, community, and church.

Education: Basic education was available to some children, particularly boys. However, access for girls and rural families varied.

Health and Medicine: Medical knowledge was limited, with high child mortality rates and frequent outbreaks of diseases like cholera.

Gender Roles: Women were expected to focus on domestic duties and childcare, though they played vital roles in supporting farms and businesses.

CULTURAL LIFE

Religion: Faith often shaped daily life. Churches served as social and spiritual hubs.

Entertainment: Social gatherings, storytelling, and community events like barn raisings were common forms of recreation.

LIFE IN 1855 WAS DEMANDING but full of community spirit, with families like Arselia's likely navigating a mix of hope and hardship as they built their lives.

IN THE 1861 CENSUS, the "W." likely stands for Wesleyan Methodist, a denomination prominent in Canada during the mid-19th century. Wesleyan Methodism was a branch of Methodism focused on personal faith, moral discipline, and social outreach, including education and temperance.

At six years old, Arselia Shannon would have been living in a small rural community in Storrington Township, Ontario, where family and religious life were deeply intertwined. She likely attended services or gatherings at a nearby church or chapel, and if her family was Wesleyan Methodist, they may have participated in Sunday school or community events organized by the church.

Her childhood in this setting would have revolved around:

Family and Faith: Religious teachings and values were a core part of upbringing, shaping daily life and social interactions.

Education: If her family valued education, she might have attended a local schoolhouse, though formal schooling varied by region and resources.

Community Life: Rural communities emphasized neighborly cooperation. Events like church picnics or harvest festivals were likely highlights.

RELIGIOUS AFFILIATION not only reflected faith but also cultural identity and community belonging during this period.

GENEALOGY ITINERARY:

Day 1: Arrival in Kingston, Ontario

• Morning: Arrive in Kingston, the nearest major city to Storrington. Check into your accommodation.

• Afternoon: Visit the Kingston Frontenac Public Library to explore their genealogy resources and local history archives.

• Evening: Take a walking tour of Kingston to get a feel for the area where Arselia might have visited or shopped.

Day 2: Exploring Storrington

• Morning: Drive to Storrington Township (now part of South Frontenac). Start at the South Frontenac Museum in Hartington to learn about the local history and see exhibits related to the 19th century

Our History | Township of South Frontenac[1]

———————

• AFTERNOON: VISIT local historical sites such as old churches and cemeteries. Look for records at the Storrington Wesleyan Methodist Church if it still exists or check local archives for church records.

• Evening: Enjoy a quiet evening in the countryside, reflecting on the day's discoveries.

Day 3: Archives and Records

• Morning: Head to the Archives of Ontario in Toronto (if you can make the trip) to access vital records, land records, and wills

Place:Storrington, Frontenac, Ontario, Canada - Genealogy[2]

———————

1. https://www.southfrontenac.net/living-in-south-frontenac/our-history/

2. https://www.werelate.org/wiki/Place:Storrington%2C_Frontenac%2C_Ontario%2C_Canada

- AFTERNOON: USE ONLINE resources at the archives or local libraries to search for birth, marriage, and death records. Websites like FamilySearch.org and Library and Archives Canada can be very helpful

https://www.bac-lac.gc.ca/eng/discover/vital-statistics-births-marriages-deaths/births-marriages-deaths-recorded/Pages/search.aspxhttps://ancestors.familysearch.org/

- EVENING: ORGANIZE your findings and plan the next steps in your research.

Day 4: Local History and Culture

- Morning: Visit the Rideau Canal and learn about its impact on the region during Arselia's time

Our History | Township of South Frontenac[3]

- AFTERNOON: EXPLORE the Frontenac Provincial Park to see the natural environment that Arselia would have known.

- Evening: Attend a local cultural event or visit a historical reenactment if available.

Day 5: Wrapping Up

- Morning: Revisit any sites or archives for follow-up research.

- Afternoon: Compile your notes and create a summary of your findings.

---

3. https://www.southfrontenac.net/living-in-south-frontenac/our-history/

- Evening: Depart from Kingston, taking with you a deeper understanding of Arselia Shannon's life and times.

Feel free to adjust this itinerary based on your specific interests and the availability of resources. Happy researching!

THOMAS SHANNON

THOMAS SHANNON[2]

Thomas Shannon, born in 1836 in Upper Canada, came into the world during a time of significant growth and transformation in the region. As a child of Upper Canada, he was part of a society still heavily influenced by British colonial governance and a largely agrarian economy. Here's a snapshot of life and the context of his early years:

Historical Context in 1836:

Political Climate: Upper Canada was experiencing tensions leading up to the Rebellions of 1837-1838, as reformers and loyalists clashed over political and land issues.

Economy: Agriculture dominated, with families working small farms. Infrastructure, including roads and mills, was developing, but life was still marked by hard labor and self-sufficiency.

Immigration: Many families of Irish, Scottish, and English descent were settling in the region, often receiving land grants in rural areas.

Education and Religion: Schools were often one-room schoolhouses, if they existed at all. Religion played a central role, with various Protestant denominations being prevalent in Upper Canada.

EARLY LIFE:

Thomas would have grown up helping with farm work from a young age, as most children did, learning skills like plowing, planting, and tending to livestock. His family likely participated in community events at a local church or market.

THOMAS SHANNON WAS just 1 year old when the Upper and Lower Canadian Rebellions took place in 1837-1838, events that significantly shaped the political landscape of what would eventually become modern Canada.

The Rebellions and Their Impact:

The Upper Canada Rebellion (1837): Led by William Lyon Mackenzie, it was a push against the ruling oligarchy, known as the Family Compact, demanding more democratic governance.

The Lower Canada Rebellion (1837-1838): Centered in what is now Quebec, this uprising was driven by tensions between French Canadian citizens and British colonial authorities.

Aftermath: Both rebellions were ultimately unsuccessful, but they highlighted the need for political reform, leading to the union of Upper and Lower Canada in 1841 and paving the way for responsible government.

FOR THOMAS:

Although too young to remember these events, the rebellions shaped the world he grew up in. By the time he was a young man, the region was navigating the changes brought by these uprisings, including discussions on governance, land use, and economic development. The legacy of this period influenced his life in Storrington, Ontario, especially as he became part of a community impacted by these pivotal events in Canadian history.

AT 12 YEARS OLD, THOMAS Shannon witnessed the establishment of the Principle of Responsible Government in 1848, a transformative event in Canadian history that would significantly shape the society he was growing up in.

Responsible Government (1848):

This principle meant that the executive council (or government) was accountable to the elected assembly rather than the colonial governor. It marked a move toward greater democracy and self-governance within the British colonies of Canada. Key figures like Robert Baldwin and Louis-Hippolyte Lafontaine championed these reforms.

Impact on Thomas's World:

Political Climate: The shift empowered local voices and helped address frustrations like those that fueled the 1837-1838 rebellions.

Community Development: It fostered better representation in local decisions, benefiting rural areas like Storrington as infrastructure and policies became more attuned to settlers' needs.

Economic Growth: The newfound political stability encouraged trade and agriculture, aligning with Thomas's future as a farmer in Upper Canada.

AT THIS AGE, THOMAS may not have fully grasped the importance of these changes, but they directly shaped the Canada he would grow up to contribute to as an adult.

AT 25 YEARS OLD IN 1861, Thomas Shannon was living as a farmer in Storrington, Ontario, married and practicing the Anglican faith.

Life in 1861:

Agriculture: As a farmer, Thomas would have been engaged in hard manual labor, cultivating crops like wheat, oats, and barley, or raising livestock. Storrington's rural community thrived on self-sustenance and small-scale trade.

Family Life: Married life would have been centered around building a household and managing the farm. Marriage often brought shared responsibilities, with spouses working together to maintain the home and land.

Religious Community: As an Anglican, Thomas would have participated in regular church services, which were central to both spiritual life and community gatherings. The church played a significant role in moral guidance and education.

HISTORICAL CONTEXT:

Canadian Census of 1861: This was the first comprehensive census conducted after the 1851 census. It reflected the growing population and economy of what was then Canada West.

Pre-Confederation Era: Canada was still six years away from Confederation in 1867. Discussions about uniting the provinces were beginning to gain traction, though they had yet to affect daily life in rural areas like Storrington.

THOMAS SHANNON'S LIFE reflected the realities of mid-19th century rural Ontario, with its blend of agricultural work, family responsibilities, and community ties through religion.

GENEALOGY ITINERARY:

Day 1: Arrival in Kingston, Ontario

• Morning: Arrive in Kingston, the nearest major city to Storrington. Check into your accommodation.

• Afternoon: Visit the Kingston Frontenac Public Library to explore their genealogy resources and local history archives.

• Evening: Take a walking tour of Kingston to get a feel for the area during Thomas Shannon's time.

Day 2: Exploring Storrington

• Morning: Drive to Storrington Township (now part of South Frontenac). Start at the South Frontenac Museum in Hartington to learn about the local history and see exhibits related to the 19th century

Place:Storrington, Frontenac, Ontario, Canada - Genealogy[1]

• AFTERNOON: VISIT local historical sites such as old churches and cemeteries. Look for records at the local Anglican Church or check local archives for church records

Archival Partners - The Anglican Church of Canada[2]

---

1. https://www.werelate.org/wiki/Place:Storrington%2C_Frontenac%2C_Ontario%2C_Canada

2. https://www.anglican.ca/archives/incanada/

• EVENING: ENJOY A quiet evening in the countryside, reflecting on the day's discoveries.

Day 3: Archives and Records

• Morning: Head to the Archives of Ontario in Toronto (if you can make the trip) to access vital records, land records, and wills

Search: Births, Marriages and Deaths recorded in Canada - Library and Archives Canada[3]

• AFTERNOON: USE ONLINE resources at the archives or local libraries to search for birth, marriage, and death records. Websites like FamilySearch.org and Library and Archives Canada can be very helpful

https://www.familysearch.org/en/wiki/Ontario_Church_Recordshttps://library-archives.canada.ca/eng/collection/research-help/genealogy-family-history/birth-marriage-death-records/pages/parish-records.aspx

---

• EVENING: ORGANIZE your findings and plan the next steps in your research.

Day 4: Local History and Culture

• Morning: Visit the Rideau Canal and learn about its impact on the region during Thomas's time

Place:Storrington, Frontenac, Ontario, Canada - Genealogy[4]

---

3. https://www.bac-lac.gc.ca/eng/discover/vital-statistics-births-marriages-deaths/births-marriages-deaths-recorded/Pages/search.aspx

4. https://www.werelate.org/wiki/Place:Storrington%2C_Frontenac%2C_Ontario%2C_Canada

• AFTERNOON: EXPLORE the Frontenac Provincial Park to see the natural environment that Thomas would have known.

• Evening: Attend a local cultural event or visit a historical reenactment if available.

Day 5: Wrapping Up

• Morning: Revisit any sites or archives for follow-up research.

• Afternoon: Compile your notes and create a summary of your findings.

• Evening: Depart from Kingston, taking with you a deeper understanding of Thomas Shannon's life and times.

Feel free to adjust this itinerary based on your specific interests and the availability of resources. Happy researching!

SARAH (UNKNOWN) SHANNON

SARAH (UNKNOWN) SHANNON[3]

Sarah Shannon, born in 1840 in Upper Canada, grew up during a time of significant political and social development in the region. By 1861, she was 21 years old, married to Thomas Shannon, living in Storrington, Ontario, and practicing the Anglican faith.

Life in 1840:

Upper Canada: In the year of Sarah's birth, Upper Canada (modern-day Ontario) was still reeling from the Upper Canada Rebellion of 1837. The aftermath saw reforms in governance and discussions about the colony's future.

Daily Life: Rural families, like the one Sarah likely grew up in, relied on agriculture for sustenance. Women were often tasked with household chores, gardening, and assisting in farming tasks from a young age.

Education: Educational opportunities were limited, especially for girls, but some basic schooling might have been available in larger settlements or through church initiatives.

LIFE IN 1861:

Marriage and Responsibilities: By 21, Sarah was married to Thomas, managing household duties, and likely assisting with farming operations. Rural wives were integral to farm life, contributing to both domestic and agricultural work.

Religious Community: As an Anglican, Sarah's life would have been closely tied to the local church, which served as both a place of worship and a hub for social interaction.

SARAH'S EARLY LIFE coincided with a transformative period in Canadian history, and by 1861, she was part of a growing community in Canada West, balancing the demands of family and farm life with her role in the Anglican community.

MELISEY CONNELL

M ELISEY CONNELL[4]

Melisey Connell, born in 1852 in Canada West (modern-day Ontario), grew up during a period of rapid growth and development in the colony. By the mid-19th century, Canada West was transitioning socially, economically, and politically, laying the groundwork for what would become Canada in 1867.

Life in 1852:

Canada West Society: The population was expanding as settlers from the British Isles and other parts of Europe arrived. Communities were largely rural, with agriculture as the primary occupation.

Living Conditions: Homes were modest, often built from timber or stone. Families relied on hard work, resourcefulness, and a strong sense of community to thrive.

Childhood Life: Children like Melisey would have grown up in a family-oriented environment, contributing to household and farm chores. Education was not universal, but she might have attended a small local school if her community had one.

IN 1861, NINE-YEAR-old Melisey Connell was living in Storrington, Ontario, and identified as Anglican according to the census. Storrington was a rural farming community, where life revolved around the rhythms of agricultural work and close-knit social and religious gatherings.

Life for a 9-Year-Old Girl in 1861:

Daily Routine: Melisey likely contributed to household chores such as cooking, cleaning, or tending to a family garden. Children her age often played a role in helping their parents manage the household or farm.

Religion: As an Anglican, she and her family would have attended services at the local parish, which was a central part of both spiritual life and social interaction within the community.

Education: While education was becoming more common, especially in Canada West, rural schooling was often limited. If there was a local school, she might have attended sporadically, balancing lessons with family responsibilities.

Community Life: Storrington in 1861 was part of a developing colony. The community was likely close-knit, with neighbors helping each other in times of need. Social gatherings were often tied to church activities or local events.

THE 1861 CENSUS CAPTURES her at a formative age, living in a colony that was steadily advancing toward Canadian Confederation just six years later.

ELISABETH SHAINON

E LISABETH SHAINON[5]

Elisabeth Shannon, born in 1840 in Upper Canada, grew up during a transformative period in Canadian history. Upper Canada was a British colony that would later become Canada West after the 1841 Act of Union.

Life in Upper Canada in 1840:

Agriculture-Based Economy: Elisabeth's family likely lived in a rural community, where farming was the primary occupation.

Social and Cultural Norms: Communities were close-knit, and societal roles were traditionally defined. Women and girls were expected to assist in household work, which included cooking, weaving, and childcare.

Education: Education opportunities were limited and varied by region. Schools were often small, church-run, or informal.

Religion: As a predominantly Protestant colony, religion played a central role in daily life, influencing everything from schooling to social events.

ELISABETH'S TIMELINE:

1841 (Age 1): The Act of Union merged Upper and Lower Canada into the Province of Canada.

1849 (Age 9): She witnessed the establishment of responsible government, giving local leaders more control over governance.

1850s: The growth of railroads and improved infrastructure began transforming the colony, increasing trade and connectivity.

ELISABETH SHANNON, born in 1840 in Upper Canada, grew up during a transformative period in Canadian history. Upper Canada was a British colony that would later become Canada West after the 1841 Act of Union.

Life in Upper Canada in 1840:

Agriculture-Based Economy: Elisabeth's family likely lived in a rural community, where farming was the primary occupation.

Social and Cultural Norms: Communities were close-knit, and societal roles were traditionally defined. Women and girls were expected to assist in household work, which included cooking, weaving, and childcare.

Education: Education opportunities were limited and varied by region. Schools were often small, church-run, or informal.

Religion: As a predominantly Protestant colony, religion played a central role in daily life, influencing everything from schooling to social events.

ELISABETH'S TIMELINE:

1841 (Age 1): The Act of Union merged Upper and Lower Canada into the Province of Canada.

1849 (Age 9): She witnessed the establishment of responsible government, giving local leaders more control over governance.

1850s: The growth of railroads and improved infrastructure began transforming the colony, increasing trade and connectivity.

IN 1861:

By this time, Elisabeth was 21 years old, likely married, or preparing for marriage, as was common for women of her age. She would have been living in Canada West, part of the thriving rural landscape of what is now Ontario, and navigating the cultural and societal expectations of young women in her community.

GENEALOGY ITINERARY:

Day 1: Arrival in Ontario

• Destination: Kingston, Ontario (nearest major city to Storrington)

• Activities:

• Settle into your accommodation.

• Visit the Kingston Public Library to gather initial information and resources.

Day 2: Exploring Birth Records

• Destination: Archives of Ontario, Toronto

• Activities:

• Search for birth records from 1840 in Upper Canada.

• Look for any baptism records in Anglican church archives.

Day 3: Storrington, Ontario

• Destination: Storrington, Ontario

• Activities:

• Visit St. Paul's Anglican Church to explore parish records.

• Walk around the area to get a sense of the place where Elisabeth lived in 1861.

Day 4: Census Records and Local History

• Destination: Kingston, Ontario

• Activities:

• Visit the Kingston Frontenac Public Library to access the 1861 Census of Canada.

• Check local history books and archives for any mentions of Elisabeth Shainon.

Day 5: Land and Property Records

• Destination: Archives of Ontario, Toronto

• Activities:

• Investigate land petitions and grants from the mid-1800s.

• Look for any property records related to Elisabeth or her family.

Day 6: Marriage and Death Records

• Destination: Kingston, Ontario

• Activities:

• Search for marriage records post-1861 in local archives.

• Look for death and burial records in church archives and public records.

Day 7: Local Historical Societies

• Destination: Various locations in Ontario

• Activities:

• Contact local historical societies in Storrington and Kingston for additional information.

• Visit any local museums or historical sites that might provide context about the era Elisabeth lived in.

Day 8: Wrap-Up and Reflection

• Destination: Kingston, Ontario

• Activities:

• Compile all gathered information and documents.

• Reflect on the journey and plan any follow-up research.

This itinerary should give you a comprehensive approach to tracing Elisabeth Shainon's genealogy while exploring the beautiful region of Ontario. Enjoy your journey into the past!

JOHN WALDRON

═══

J OHN WALDRON[6]

John Waldron, born in Ireland in 1805, grew up during a period of profound social, political, and economic change.

Life in Ireland, 1805:

Rural Setting: Most Irish families lived in rural areas, with farming being a primary occupation. The agricultural system was often exploitative, with tenant farmers working small plots of land owned by absentee landlords.

Population Growth: Ireland was experiencing significant population growth, which, coupled with reliance on the potato as a staple food, made life precarious for many.

British Rule: Ireland was under British control, and 1805 was during the Napoleonic Wars, a time of political tension. Irish citizens had limited representation and rights, leading to unrest in subsequent years.

Cultural Traditions: Irish culture remained rich, with oral storytelling, music, and Catholic religious practices as integral aspects of daily life.

═══

JOHN WALDRON WAS 12 years old in 1817, the year the bicycle (specifically the "Draisine" or "running machine") was invented by Baron Karl von Drais in Germany.

This early version of the bicycle, made entirely of wood and lacking pedals, sparked innovation in personal transportation. While it likely didn't have a direct impact on rural Ireland at the time, it represented the kind of technological advances that would slowly shape the world John lived in.

———

JOHN WALDRON WAS 21 years old in 1826, the year John Walker, an English chemist, invented the first friction matches. These early matches were a significant innovation, making fire-starting much easier and more portable than previous methods like flint and steel or chemical reactions.

For someone in rural Ireland like John, this invention might not have been immediately accessible, but it marked the beginning of a shift toward more modern conveniences that would eventually reach even remote areas. Matches became a game-changer for everyday life, especially in farming communities reliant on fire for cooking, heating, and lighting.

———

IN 1861, JOHN WALDRON, at the age of 56, was living in Storrington, Ontario, where he worked as a farmer. As a married man and an Anglican, his life likely revolved around his family, the Anglican Church, and the daily demands of farm work.

Storrington in this period was a rural township in Canada West (modern Ontario), characterized by a close-knit community where agriculture was the primary livelihood. Being an Anglican suggests that John and his family were part of a well-established religious tradition, with services and social gatherings likely held at a local parish church. Life on the farm would have involved hard work, from tending crops and livestock to preparing for the long Canadian winters.

GENEALOGY ITINERARY:

Day 1: Arrival in Ontario

• Destination: Kingston, Ontario (nearest major city to Storrington)

• Activities:

• Settle into your accommodation.

• Visit the Kingston Public Library to gather initial information and resources.

Day 2: Exploring Birth Records

• Destination: Archives of Ontario, Toronto

• Activities:

• Search for birth records from 1805 in Ireland.

• Look for any baptism records in Anglican church archives.

Day 3: Storrington, Ontario

• Destination: Storrington, Ontario

• Activities:

• Visit St. Paul's Anglican Church to explore parish records

Archives | Resources | Anglican Diocese of Ontario[1]

• WALK AROUND THE AREA to get a sense of the place where John lived in 1861.

Day 4: Census Records and Local History

---

1. https://ontario.anglican.ca/resources/archives

- Destination: Kingston, Ontario

- Activities:

- Visit the Kingston Frontenac Public Library to access the 1861 Census of Canada

Ontario Church Records • FamilySearch[2]

- CHECK LOCAL HISTORY books and archives for any mentions of John Waldron.

Day 5: Land and Property Records

- Destination: Archives of Ontario, Toronto

- Activities:

- Investigate land petitions and grants from the mid-1800s

to the Ontario Land Records Index Microfiche[3]

- LOOK FOR ANY PROPERTY records related to John or his family

Search land property records | ontario.ca[4]

DAY 6: MARRIAGE AND Death Records

- Destination: Kingston, Ontario

2. https://www.familysearch.org/en/wiki/Ontario_Church_Records

3. https://www.archives.gov.on.ca/en/microfilm/crown_land_records_microfiche.aspx

4. https://www.ontario.ca/page/search-land-property-records

• Activities:

• Search for marriage records post-1861 in local archives.

• Look for death and burial records in church archives and public records

<u>Parish and related birth, marriage and death records</u>[5]

DAY 7: LOCAL HISTORICAL Societies

• Destination: Various locations in Ontario

• Activities:

• Contact local historical societies in Storrington and Kingston for additional information.

• Visit any local museums or historical sites that might provide context about the era John lived in.

Day 8: Wrap-Up and Reflection

• Destination: Kingston, Ontario

• Activities:

• Compile all gathered information and documents.

• Reflect on the journey and plan any follow-up research.

This itinerary should give you a comprehensive approach to tracing John Waldron's genealogy while exploring the beautiful region of Ontario.

---

5. https://library-archives.canada.ca/eng/collection/research-help/genealogy-family-history/birth-marriage-death-records/pages/parish-records.aspx

SUSAN (UNKNOWN) WALDRON

S USAN (UNKNOWN) WALDRON[7]

Susan Waldron, born in Scotland in 1805, shared the same birth year as her husband, John. By 1861, she was 56 years old, married, and living in Storrington, Ontario. As an Anglican, she likely participated in the church community alongside her husband.

Having emigrated from Scotland, Susan would have brought elements of her Scottish heritage to her life in Canada, influencing her household and possibly contributing traditional customs to the rural Storrington community. Daily life for her would have been filled with managing the household, supporting farm operations, and caring for her family, all while adapting to the challenges of life in 19th-century rural Canada.

SUSAN WALDRON WAS 21 years old in 1826 when matches were invented. This innovation, particularly friction matches, marked a significant turning point in daily life. The ability to easily produce fire transformed household tasks, such as lighting stoves, candles, and lamps, making them far more convenient. For someone like Susan, who would later establish a home in Canada, matches would have been a valuable tool as she navigated the challenges of domestic life in the 19th century.

SUSAN WALDRON WAS 38 years old in 1843 when A Christmas Carol by Charles Dickens was first published. This iconic novella, which quickly became a Christmas classic, was widely embraced for its moral lessons about generosity, compassion, and the spirit of Christmas. In the context of her life, living in Canada during a period of growth and change, Susan would have witnessed how Dickens' works resonated with the emerging middle class in both the United Kingdom and the colonies. The themes of redemption and familial bonds in A Christmas Carol may have echoed through the lives of many immigrants like Susan, adjusting to a new land while cherishing traditions.

SUSAN WALDRON WAS 41 years old in 1846 when Elias Howe patented the first practical sewing machine. This invention revolutionized the textile industry, dramatically increasing production speeds and efficiency, and soon found its way into homes, changing the way people sewed clothing. For someone like Susan, living in Storrington, Ontario, this innovation would have been a significant development, especially for women who often spent a great deal of time sewing for their families. It might have also had an impact on the local economy and could have been a source of employment or opportunity as the new technology spread throughout communities.

IN 1861, SUSAN WALDRON, at 56 years old, was living in Storrington, Ontario, and was listed as Anglican. At this stage in her life, she would have been deeply integrated into the fabric of her community, likely contributing to her family's farm and household.

Given the time period, Susan would have witnessed numerous changes during her lifetime: the growth of Upper Canada into the Province of Ontario, the shift from agrarian to more industrial economies in certain areas, and the increasingly widespread use of innovations like the sewing machine, which would have affected domestic life. As a member of the Anglican faith, she would have participated in the religious and social structures of the community, and in rural Ontario, she may have also had a role in local charitable work or social gatherings within her church.

At 56, Susan may have been looking after a growing family, possibly with older children of her own, and could have had an influential role in shaping the family's traditions and values.

THOMAS WALDRON

THOMAS WALDRON[8]

In 1836, when Thomas Waldron was born in Frontenac, Upper Canada, the region was still experiencing the early stages of its development. Life in Upper Canada (now Ontario) was shaped by a mix of colonial governance, pioneer farming, and growing unrest leading up to the Upper Canada Rebellion of 1837.

Social and Political Climate

Colonial Rule: Upper Canada was a British colony governed by a small, elite group known as the Family Compact, which controlled much of the political and economic power. Many settlers felt excluded and were becoming increasingly frustrated with the lack of democratic representation, setting the stage for rebellion.

Land Settlements: Many families in the area were pioneers who had received land grants or purchased land to clear for farming. Settlers worked hard to establish homesteads in a landscape dominated by forests and waterways.

DAILY LIFE

Farming: Families like the Waldrons likely focused on subsistence farming, growing crops such as wheat, barley, and oats while keeping livestock. Most daily activities revolved around survival—building homes, clearing land, and tending crops and animals.

Transportation: Roads were minimal, often little more than trails through the woods. Rivers and lakes were the primary means of transportation, especially in Frontenac County, which is part of the Rideau Canal system completed just four years earlier, in 1832.

Community Life: Settlements were scattered, and social life often centered on church services or gatherings for barn raisings or other cooperative tasks. Education and medical care were rudimentary and often unavailable in rural areas.

HISTORICAL CONTEXT

Indigenous Relations: Settlers were living on land that had long been home to Indigenous peoples, whose lives were increasingly disrupted by European settlement and treaties that ceded territory to the Crown.

Immigration and Growth: Upper Canada was rapidly growing due to immigration, particularly from Ireland and Scotland, as well as Loyalists from the United States. This influx of settlers brought diverse cultures and labor, fueling the expansion of communities like Frontenac.

IN THIS ENVIRONMENT, Thomas would have grown up experiencing the hard work and resilience required to build a life in a developing colony, surrounded by the rich natural resources and challenges of the Canadian wilderness. By the time of his birth, his family would have been adapting to the demands of pioneer life while looking forward to a more stable future in the growing colony.

AT 11 YEARS OLD, THOMAS Waldron witnessed the establishment of the principles of responsible government in 1847, which marked a turning point in Canadian political history. While he may not have fully understood its implications at the time, the events around this change would have shaped the world he grew up in.

What Happened in 1847?

Responsible Government: This principle meant that elected representatives, rather than appointed officials or colonial governors, would hold more authority in making decisions. It laid the foundation for the parliamentary democracy we know today. The shift was spearheaded by reform leaders like Robert Baldwin and Louis-Hippolyte Lafontaine.

Impact on Upper Canada: In Upper Canada, this move toward self-governance meant more direct representation of settlers' needs, such as better infrastructure, land rights, and local laws, which were crucial to families like the Waldrons.

***

HOW THIS AFFECTED FAMILIES Like the Waldrons

Improved Governance: Local settlers began to feel more heard as elected officials took greater control over legislative matters. This would eventually improve public services like schools, roads, and mail delivery—although these changes took time to reach rural areas like Frontenac.

Greater Stability: The promise of a more democratic system likely reassured settlers about their future in the colony, encouraging them to invest further in their land and communities.

***

WHILE YOUNG THOMAS might not have been directly involved in political matters, the introduction of responsible government contributed to a more stable and hopeful environment for settlers, shaping the Canada he would grow up to live and work in.

———

IN 1861, 24-YEAR-OLD Thomas Waldron was a farmer and Anglican, living in Storrington Township, Ontario. This was a time when agriculture dominated rural life, and young men like Thomas often worked tirelessly to maintain their family farms.

Life in 1861 for Farmers in Storrington

Agricultural Focus: Farming involved long days of manual labor, including plowing, planting, and harvesting crops like wheat, barley, and oats. Livestock farming, including cattle and pigs, was also common.

Tools and Techniques: Farmers relied on horse- or oxen-drawn equipment, as mechanized tools like the reaper and threshing machine were just starting to become more widespread.

Community Life: Anglican families like the Waldrons would gather at church for Sunday worship, which served as both a spiritual and social hub.

Infrastructure: By 1861, Storrington had developed modest infrastructure, including basic schools, local markets, and dirt roads connecting farms to nearby towns like Kingston.

———

THE 1861 CENSUS CONTEXT

The 1861 Census of Canada was the first to document the population of the Province of Canada (comprising modern-day Ontario and Quebec). As a farmer, Thomas's household would have been surveyed for details on their land, livestock, and produce, offering a snapshot of his economic and social standing.

Thomas was part of a generation helping to shape rural Ontario, balancing the hard work of farming with the traditions and faith of his Anglican upbringing.

GENEALOGY ITINERARY:

Day 1: Arrival in Kingston, Ontario

• Morning: Arrive in Kingston, Ontario. Check into your hotel and rest after your journey.

• Afternoon: Visit the Frontenac County Archives to explore birth records and other documents related to Thomas Waldron's early life in Frontenac, Upper Canada.

• Evening: Enjoy dinner at a local restaurant in Kingston's historic downtown area.

Day 2: Exploring Frontenac County

• Morning: Travel to the rural areas of Frontenac County where Thomas Waldron was born. Visit local Anglican churches and cemeteries to find records and graves of the Waldron family.

• Afternoon: Meet with local historians or genealogists to gain insights into the area during the 1830s.

• Evening: Return to Kingston and relax.

Day 3: Storrington, Ontario

• Morning: Travel to Storrington, Ontario. Visit the local Anglican church where Thomas Waldron was recorded in the 1861 census. Explore church records and speak with current church members about its history.

• Afternoon: Visit local cemeteries to find Thomas Waldron's grave and pay your respects.

• Evening: Return to Kingston and enjoy dinner at a local restaurant.

Day 4: Kingston and Local Archives

• Morning: Visit the Kingston Frontenac Public Library and the Queen's University Archives to research more about Thomas Waldron's life and work in Ontario.

• Afternoon: Explore Kingston's historic sites, such as Fort Henry and the Kingston Penitentiary, to get a sense of the area's history during Thomas Waldron's time.

• Evening: Reflect on your journey and the life of Thomas Waldron over dinner.

Day 5: Departure

• Morning: Check out of your hotel and travel back to Toronto.

• Afternoon: Fly back home, carrying with you the memories and discoveries of your genealogical journey.

This itinerary should provide a meaningful and comprehensive way to honor Thomas Waldron's life and legacy

GORDON WALDRON

GORDON WALDRON[9]

Gordon Waldron was born in 1839 in Upper Canada (modern-day Ontario), during a time of significant growth and transformation in the colony.

Life in 1839

Rural Environment: Upper Canada was primarily rural, with settlers like the Waldrons engaged in farming or small-scale industry. New communities were forming, and roads were gradually improving to connect settlements.

Rebellion Aftermath: Gordon's birth year coincided with the aftermath of the Upper and Lower Canadian Rebellions (1837-1838), which called for political reform. These events contributed to the eventual establishment of responsible government.

Family and Community: Families like the Waldrons relied heavily on cooperation and community ties for survival, from building homes to harvesting crops.

GORDON WAS BORN INTO a world where the traditions of colonial life were starting to shift toward a more structured, self-governed society. This formative period would influence the opportunities and challenges he faced as he grew up in a farming family.

WHEN GORDON WALDRON was 5 years old, his sister Jane Anne Waldron was born in April 1844 in Upper Canada. At this time, the Waldron family was likely well-established in their rural life, continuing to build their farmstead and contribute to their local community.

For Gordon, the arrival of a younger sibling would have been a significant event, adding to the responsibilities of older children in helping care for the household and farm. Jane Anne's birth in 1844 came during a period of social and economic stability in Upper Canada, as political reforms and infrastructural improvements were beginning to reshape life in the colony.

WHEN GORDON WALDRON was 9 years old in 1848, the Principle of Responsible Government was established in Canada. This was a transformative time in the colonies, as this principle marked a shift toward more democratic governance, where elected officials in the legislature held greater accountability to the public rather than solely to colonial governors.

For Gordon, living in Upper Canada, this political shift may not have directly impacted his daily life on the farm, but it was a time of change that influenced the community and society around him. Local newspapers and discussions in churches or marketplaces would have spread news of these developments, introducing ideas of governance and reform to rural areas. These events helped shape the foundations of the self-governing nation Gordon and his family were part of.

IN 1861, GORDON WALDRON, at 22 years old, was single and living at home with his family in Storrington Township, Ontario. He was Anglican and worked as a farmer, contributing to the daily operations of the family farm.

This would have been a busy life, marked by long days tending crops, caring for livestock, and maintaining the land. As a young, unmarried man in a rural farming community, Gordon's responsibilities likely revolved around supporting his parents, John and Susan Waldron, and helping ensure the farm's productivity. In the growing township of Storrington, religion and community were central to daily life, and Gordon's Anglican faith would have provided spiritual guidance and a sense of belonging.

JANE ANNE WALDRON

JANE ANNE WALDRON[10]

Jane Anne Waldron was born in Ontario, Upper Canada, in April 1844. As the youngest in the Waldron family, her early years were likely spent in the rural surroundings of Storrington Township, where she would have been raised in a close-knit farming household.

By the time of her birth, Upper Canada (now part of Ontario) was experiencing social and political changes, including the push for responsible government. Life in rural Ontario was centered on farming, with families working together to sustain their livelihoods. Jane Anne would have grown up learning domestic and agricultural tasks, typical for young girls in a farming community during the mid-19th century. Family values and the Anglican faith would have been significant influences in her upbringing.

JANE ANNE WALDRON WAS 3 years old when the Principles of Responsible Government were established in 1847, marking an important shift in Canadian political history. This milestone, which granted colonies like Upper Canada more autonomy in self-governance, laid the groundwork for the democratic processes that would shape the future of Ontario.

Though Jane Anne would have been too young to comprehend the significance of these changes, her formative years unfolded in a time of growing political maturity in Canada. These developments likely influenced her family's discussions and outlook on life, particularly as they farmed and worshiped in Storrington Township, adapting to the evolving landscape of mid-19th-century Ontario.

IN 1861, JANE ANNE Waldron was 16 years old, Anglican, and living with her family in Storrington, Ontario. As a young woman of her time, she would likely have taken on domestic responsibilities within her household while helping to maintain the family farm.

Her life revolved around the rhythms of rural Ontario—attending church services, participating in community events, and contributing to the family's self-sufficiency. Being Anglican, her family likely attended regular services and followed traditions that tied them to the broader British colonial culture of the period. At 16, Jane Anne was on the cusp of adulthood in an era when young women often began to prepare for marriage and family life.

ELISABETH WALDRON

———

E LISABETH WALDRON[11]

Elisabeth Waldron was born in Upper Canada in 1835, making her the eldest sibling in the family. As the first-born child, she likely took on a leadership role in the household, especially given the nature of family life during that time. Being born into a rural, predominantly Anglican community, Elisabeth would have been raised with a strong sense of responsibility toward family and church.

———

ELISABETH WALDRON WOULD have been 2 years old during the Upper and Lower Canada Rebellions of 1837-1838. These rebellions were significant events in the history of Canada as the colonists, both in Upper Canada (Ontario) and Lower Canada (Quebec), sought more autonomy from British rule. As a young child, Elisabeth wouldn't have understood the full political implications, but the turmoil and changes in the colony would have likely had an indirect effect on her early life.

———

ELISABETH WALDRON WOULD have been 13 years old when the Principles of Responsible Government were established in 1848. This period marked a significant shift in Canada's political landscape. Responsible government allowed for elected representatives to have real power in decision-making, replacing the old system where the British-appointed governor had control.

For Elisabeth, living in Upper Canada at that time, this would have been a period of growing political awareness and a shift towards more local autonomy from British colonial rule, which would shape the future of her community and the country as a whole.

BY 1861, ELISABETH was 26 years old, and as the eldest daughter, she likely played an important part in managing the domestic tasks and caring for younger siblings. Depending on her circumstances, she may have been married by this time, or she could have been preparing for marriage, as young women in this era often did. Given the focus on self-sufficiency and community ties, Elisabeth would have been accustomed to hard work on the family farm and may have been an active participant in local church activities as well.

SAMUEL W. WATTERS

SAMUEL W. WATTERS[12]

Samuel W. Watters was born in Ireland in 1824, during a period marked by political unrest and societal changes. Ireland was under British rule, and many Irish people faced difficult conditions, including poverty, land issues, and social inequality. The early 1800s in Ireland were also shaped by the aftermath of the Napoleonic Wars and the Great Irish Famine, which would have occurred later, in the mid-1840s.

Samuel's birth in 1824 places him in a generation that witnessed the rise of Irish nationalism, including movements for Irish independence and better living conditions. He would have likely grown up during a time when the Irish population was facing significant hardships, which may have influenced his later decisions, including immigration.

By the time Samuel immigrated to Canada, Ireland's challenges had sparked the migration of many Irish people seeking better opportunities in places like Canada, where farmland and religious freedom were important draws. This sets the stage for his eventual life in Canada, potentially in a community like Storrington, Ontario.

SAMUEL WATTERS, BORN in 1824, was 2 years old in 1826, the year the first practical match was invented by John Walker, an English chemist. Before the invention of matches, lighting a fire was a much more labor-intensive process, typically requiring flint and steel or a slow-burning tinderbox. The creation of the match revolutionized everyday life, making it easier and safer for people to start fires for cooking, heating, and light. This invention would have likely been a part of the technological advancements Samuel would have experienced as he grew older.

THE IRISH HURRICANE occurred in 1839, making Samuel Watters 15 years old at the time. This powerful storm, also known as the "Great Storm of 1839," caused significant damage across Ireland, particularly in coastal areas, with strong winds, heavy rains, and widespread flooding. For someone of Samuel's age, living in Ireland, the hurricane would have been a memorable and possibly frightening event, especially as it severely impacted both the environment and people's lives. The event likely left an impression on him, as it was a natural disaster that shook communities and caused lasting disruptions during that time.

SAMUEL WATTERS WAS 21 years old during the Irish Famine immigration of 1845, a pivotal moment in Irish history. The famine, caused by a potato blight, led to widespread starvation and death, triggering a mass exodus of Irish people seeking a better life abroad, particularly to Canada, the United States, and Britain.

As a young adult in Ireland, Samuel would have witnessed firsthand the devastating effects of the famine on his community and country. The large wave of Irish immigration in the mid-1800s drastically changed the demographic makeup of many regions, including Canada, where many Irish immigrants settled. Samuel, at 21, might have been directly affected by this migration, either through his own decision to emigrate or by witnessing the challenges faced by family members, friends, or neighbors who chose to leave Ireland in search of better opportunities.

AT 31 YEARS OLD, SAMUEL Watters had established himself in Canada West (now Ontario) by 1855, a time when the area was undergoing significant social and economic development. Samuel's son, also named Samuel, was born during a period of growth and change for the region. Canada West was experiencing agricultural expansion, with many settlers working the land, particularly through farming, which would have likely been the livelihood of the Watters family.

During this time, the population of Canada West was growing rapidly, partly due to the influx of immigrants, including those from Ireland like Samuel. The early 1850s also saw a focus on improving infrastructure, like roads and railways, which would have benefited farmers and settlers like Samuel. The birth of his son could have marked a moment of optimism and hope for the future, as the family looked forward to the opportunities of life in the growing province.

AT 33 YEARS OLD IN 1857, Samuel Watters would have experienced the continuing transformation of Canada West. By this time, the region was becoming more settled, with the population steadily increasing as more immigrants arrived, especially from Ireland, as well as from other parts of Europe. Samuel's son, William, was born during a time when the economy of Canada West was thriving, with agriculture being a major sector. The availability of fertile land for farming offered opportunities for families like the Watters to grow and prosper.

In 1857, Canada West was also seeing a boom in infrastructure development, including the expansion of the railroads and the growth of towns and cities. This would have provided new opportunities for commerce, transportation, and trade, which may have impacted Samuel's life and his family's prospects. As a father, the birth of William would have been seen as part of the family's future in a rapidly evolving landscape, with the promise of prosperity and stability in a growing and developing society.

IN 1861, SAMUEL WATTERS, now 37 years old, was a farmer in Storrington, Ontario. As an Irish Presbyterian, he would have been part of a vibrant community of immigrants who had settled in Canada West, seeking new opportunities and a better life after the hardships faced in Ireland. This was a period of considerable growth and expansion in the region, with agriculture as the backbone of the local economy.

The Irish community in Storrington, like many others across Ontario, had a significant influence on the development of the area, contributing not only to the economy through farming but also to the social and religious fabric. Samuel's Presbyterian faith would have been central to his family's life, with church gatherings being an important part of the community. As a farmer, he likely worked the land with the help of his family, cultivating crops and raising livestock to support his household.

By 1861, Samuel had lived through the tumultuous years of his youth, the Irish immigration of the 1840s, and the rapid development of Ontario. His life would have been one of hard work and perseverance, with his family's future tied to the land they worked. The rise of local industry, the growth of transportation networks like the railway, and the expansion of towns would have also created new possibilities for Samuel and his children in the years to come.

MARY M. (UNKNOWN) WATTERS

———

M ARY M. (UNKNOWN) WATTERS[13]

Mary, born in 1824 in Ireland, grew up during a time of significant social, political, and economic upheaval. The early 19th century in Ireland was marked by harsh conditions for the majority of the population, particularly for the Irish peasantry. The early 1800s were still under British rule, and Ireland was experiencing a period of political unrest, leading to events like the 1798 Irish Rebellion. By the time Mary was born, Ireland had been through a series of economic depressions, and much of the country's population was living in poverty.

The Irish Great Famine, which began in 1845, was a defining event in the lives of many Irish families, and it is likely that Mary, like many others, faced difficult conditions. The famine caused widespread crop failures, particularly the failure of the potato crop on which many Irish peasants relied for food. It led to mass starvation, disease, and the death of approximately one million people. In addition, millions were forced to emigrate, fleeing the famine in hopes of finding a better life abroad. It's very likely that Mary and her family were among those who sought a new life in Canada, as many Irish immigrants did during this period.

Life for Mary would have been challenging, and it's possible she was one of the many Irish women who worked hard on family farms, in homes, or in small industries. She would have faced the same struggles as other Irish women of her time, dealing with poverty, the harsh realities of rural life, and the oppressive systems in place under British colonial rule. If she emigrated to Canada in her youth or as a young adult, she would have faced the significant challenges of adapting to life in a new land, far from the support systems of Ireland.

The early years of their marriage with Samuel in Storrington would have likely been centered around survival and building a new life in Canada. As a farmer's wife, she would have been responsible for a range of household duties, including cooking, cleaning, caring for children, and managing the home, alongside the seasonal farmwork. Her faith as a Presbyterian would have provided her with comfort and a sense of community in a new land, especially as she navigated the difficulties of raising a family far from Ireland. Life for Mary would have been hard, but it was also a time when strong community ties and faith were central to everyday survival.

SAMUEL H. WATTERS

SAMUEL H. WATTERS[14]

Samuel H. Watters, born in 1855 in Canada West (now Ontario), was part of a generation that came into the world during a period of profound change. In 1855, Canada West was still part of the British colony of the Province of Canada, which had not yet confederated with the other provinces to form Canada. The province was undergoing significant social and economic transformations.

For Samuel's parents, particularly those who had emigrated from Ireland, life in Canada West offered a chance for new beginnings. While the early 1850s were relatively peaceful in comparison to the famine years, life was still difficult for many settlers. Most immigrants, like Samuel's family, would have been involved in agriculture. Samuel's father, Samuel Watters, would have likely worked as a farmer, a common occupation at the time, especially in rural Ontario, which was being cleared for farming. Farming families in Canada West often lived off the land, growing crops and raising livestock to survive, while also contributing to the economy of the fledgling colony.

The year 1855 also marked a time when many Irish immigrants were still grappling with the aftermath of the Great Famine, which had begun a decade earlier. Samuel's parents, having endured the hardships of famine and emigration, likely sought stability for their family in Canada West. The colony's population was growing rapidly during this period, especially with the continued influx of immigrants from Ireland, Scotland, and England, many of whom, like Samuel's family, were settling in rural Ontario.

Socially, Samuel would have been born into a predominantly British Protestant society. His family, being Presbyterian, would have been part of the significant Protestant population in Canada West, but they may have lived in a community where Irish Catholics were also prevalent, given the large number of Irish immigrants at the time. Religion would have played a significant role in Samuel's early life, as his family and their community gathered for worship and social interaction, helping to form the bonds that would carry them through the difficulties of pioneer life.

Samuel would have grown up during a time when Canada West was on the brink of a major shift, as the Province of Canada was edging toward confederation. In 1867, just 12 years after his birth, Canada would become a self-governing dominion within the British Empire, a momentous event that would alter the future of the region and its people. For Samuel, this change in governance might have been far removed from his daily life on the farm, but as he grew older, he would have witnessed the increasing effects of political and economic changes sweeping through Canada.

SAMUEL H. WATTERS, born in 1855, would have been two years old when his brother, William, was born in 1857 in Canada West. During this time, the family would have been settling into their life in rural Ontario, likely living a subsistence farming lifestyle. With Samuel being so young and William just born, the family would have been focused on growing crops and taking care of livestock.

Family life in the 1850s in Canada West was centered around the home, with both parents working together to raise children and manage their farm. Samuel would have grown up in a close-knit family environment, where the bond between siblings, especially brothers, would have been significant, as they would have worked together on the farm as they grew older.

The challenges of pioneer life were still present, but by 1857, Canada West was becoming more established, and the region was benefiting from the expanding infrastructure and development spurred by the influx of immigrants. Samuel and William's childhoods would have been shaped by this developing society, along with the prevailing British colonial system, religious life, and the agricultural work that formed the backbone of the community.

For Samuel, having a younger brother would have brought both joy and new responsibilities, as he would likely have helped in caring for and looking after William as he grew. The siblings would have grown up together in an environment where hard work, family, and community were central to life.

SAMUEL H. WATTERS, born in 1855, would have been four years old when his brother Thomas was born in 1859. During this time, the Watters family would have continued adapting to life in rural Ontario. Samuel would have been old enough to start helping with farm work and likely taking on small responsibilities around the home, such as fetching water, feeding animals, or assisting with younger siblings.

The arrival of Thomas would have been another significant milestone for Samuel, as he would begin to develop a stronger sense of responsibility as an older sibling. The Watters family, particularly in this rural setting, would have worked together to maintain their livelihood and support each other. Samuel would have witnessed the growth of his family, and his bond with his brothers, especially as they all grew older, would likely have played an important role in shaping his childhood.

By this time, life in Canada West was becoming more stable for settlers, but the challenges of raising a young family in a rural, agricultural environment remained. Samuel and his siblings would have likely had a close-knit relationship, working together on the farm and supporting one another.

IN 1861, AT THE AGE of 6, Samuel H. Watters would have been a young child growing up in Storrington, Ontario. The Watters family, being Presbyterian, would have been part of a close-knit religious community, where church services and community events played a central role in daily life. Samuel, as a child, would have been learning about his faith, perhaps attending Sunday school or church with his parents and siblings.

Life in Storrington during this period was rural and centered around farming. The family would have likely been working hard to maintain their livelihood, growing crops and raising animals. Samuel, at such a young age, would have mostly been observing and perhaps helping with simple tasks, learning from his parents and older siblings. His life would have been shaped by the cycles of the seasons, farming routines, and family bonds.

Presbyterianism, as part of the broader religious and cultural life of Ontario at the time, would have influenced Samuel's values and upbringing. His family would have taught him the principles of their faith, preparing him for the roles and responsibilities that would come with adulthood in a rural community.

WILLIAM W. WATTERS

W ILLIAM W. WATTERS[15]

In 1857, William Watters was born in Canada West (now Ontario), a time when the region was undergoing significant changes. Canada West was still largely rural, with settlers continuing to establish themselves in farming communities. William, like his siblings, would have been raised in a household focused on agricultural work, with his family likely involved in growing crops, raising livestock, and managing daily tasks on their farm.

Being born in Canada West meant William was part of a growing and developing area, especially as the population was increasing due to both British immigration and the establishment of more communities. The mid-1800s was also a time of significant political and social changes in Canada, with movements toward more responsible government and the eventual Confederation of Canada in 1867.

As a child, William would have been shaped by his family's Presbyterian faith and the strong sense of community that religion brought. Given the close-knit nature of rural life in the area, he would have grown up in an environment where family and neighbors were central to daily existence. Like his older brother Samuel, William's upbringing would have been marked by the responsibilities of rural life, with a strong emphasis on hard work, faith, and community values.

WILLIAM WATTERS WAS born in 1857, and his brother Thomas was born in 1859, which means William was 2 years old when Thomas arrived. Growing up in a rural family in Canada West, this would have been a time when William would have been beginning to experience the responsibilities of farm life, even if only in small ways for now. With Thomas being just a toddler, William might have been helping with basic tasks around the farm, as older siblings often took on small duties while their younger siblings were cared for by parents.

The years between 1857 and 1859 saw Canada West continue its growth, with settlers continuing to arrive, establishing farms, and developing the local economy. It was a time of expansion and gradual progress for the young Canadian province. Family life would have been marked by a strong sense of community, often centered around church activities, farming, and helping one another. As they grew, the Watters family would have seen the development of towns and improved infrastructure, bringing further opportunities.

IN 1861, WILLIAM WATTERS was 4 years old and living in Storrington, Ontario. At that time, Ontario was in the midst of significant development. Storrington, a rural area in Frontenac County, would have had a close-knit farming community. Life in the early 1860s would have been focused on agricultural work, with families growing their own food, raising livestock, and contributing to local economies.

William, being a child, would likely have been at home with his family, playing and helping with small tasks around the farm as he grew. Children in rural Ontario during this period often contributed to daily life by helping with chores, though they still had time to play outside. They were raised with a strong sense of community and family, with neighbors often relying on one another for assistance, especially in the case of harvests or special events.

The Watters family, being Presbyterian, would have also been part of a religious community. Sundays might have been spent attending church, which was an important part of social life in rural Ontario at the time. As a child, William's world would have been shaped by the rhythms of farm life, community gatherings, and the influence of his family and church.

THOMAS W. WATTERS

THOMAS W. WATTERS[16]

In 1859, Canada West (now Ontario) was a growing region undergoing significant change. Life in Canada West during this time was primarily rural, with farming being the dominant way of life. Many settlers, including the Watters family, lived on farms that produced grain, livestock, and other agricultural goods. The landscape would have been dotted with small farming communities, forests, and rivers, as much of the land was still being cleared for settlement.

Canada West was still a relatively new province, having joined the British colonies in 1841 as part of the Province of Canada (before becoming Ontario in 1867 with Confederation). The population in Canada West was growing steadily due to both immigration and the natural increase in birth rates. Immigrants, particularly from Ireland and Scotland, had settled in large numbers, bringing with them their agricultural expertise and cultural traditions.

In the mid-19th century, technology was also beginning to change the way people lived. Railways were expanding, connecting cities and rural areas, which made transportation and trade more efficient. This was an exciting time, as communities were becoming more integrated, and economic opportunities were opening up, particularly in farming, lumbering, and other industries.

For a child born in 1859 in Canada West, life would have been shaped by the rhythms of farm work, the seasons, and the influence of religion and community. Children were often expected to help with chores from a young age, and families often worked together to ensure their survival, particularly during harsh winters.

Education was available, though rural schools were often small and basic. The majority of families would have been members of a church, such as the Presbyterian Church, and the church played an important social and cultural role, often serving as the center for social activities and community gatherings.

In short, life in Canada West in 1859 was shaped by rural living, family ties, agriculture, and a growing sense of national identity as the province moved toward Confederation just a few years later.

IN 1861, THOMAS W. Watters was 2 years old and living in Storrington, Ontario. Like his siblings, Thomas would have been growing up in a rural, agricultural community, with life centered around the family farm. At this time, Ontario was still largely rural, with most families engaged in farming, fishing, and small-scale trades.

For a young child like Thomas, his world would have been primarily focused on his immediate family, home, and the natural environment. At the age of two, he would likely have been learning basic skills, perhaps starting to walk, talk, and explore the surrounding woods and fields with his family.

With his family being Presbyterian, religious teachings would also play an important part in his upbringing, and church attendance would be an integral part of community life. In this rural setting, the Watters family would have also likely relied on neighbors for support, whether for social activities or when help was needed for harvests or other communal tasks.

For a child like Thomas in the early 1860s, life in Storrington would have been shaped by the pace of nature and the rhythms of farm life, with a strong connection to family and community.

EMY HOBBS

E MY HOBBS[17]

Emy Hobbs was born in Ireland in 1842. In 1842, Ireland was under British rule and characterized by a largely agrarian economy. The population was predominantly rural, with most people relying on agriculture for survival. Tenant farming was the norm, with land owned by landlords and worked by Irish tenant families. Life was challenging, as many families lived in poverty, and their livelihoods were vulnerable to crop failures and economic changes.

At this time, Ireland was relatively peaceful, though social tensions persisted due to economic inequality and political dissatisfaction. The Catholic Emancipation of 1829 had granted Catholics the right to vote and hold political office, but significant inequalities remained between the Protestant landowning class and the Catholic majority.

1842 was just a few years before the Great Irish Famine (1845–1852), a devastating period that reshaped Irish society. The reliance on the potato as a staple food was high, particularly among the rural poor. When the potato blight struck, it led to widespread starvation and mass emigration. Though Emy Hobbs was too young to fully grasp the challenges of 1842, she would have grown up amidst the societal upheaval caused by the famine, which may have influenced her family's decision to emigrate to Canada.

For children like Emy in 1842 Ireland, life would have been centered around family, faith, and survival. Education was limited, especially for girls, though national schools were beginning to be established under British reforms. Religious practice was a cornerstone of daily life, with many families devoutly Catholic or Protestant, depending on their region and background. These experiences would have shaped Emy's early years before her journey to Canada.

AT JUST 3 YEARS OLD, Emy Hobbs would have been too young to fully understand the monumental events unfolding during the Irish immigration wave of 1845. This period marked the beginning of mass emigration caused by the Great Irish Famine, triggered by the devastating failure of the potato crop, a staple food for much of the population.

Though still a child, Emy's family may have already been feeling the effects of economic hardship, rising food prices, and declining agricultural yields. Many Irish families, particularly tenant farmers, faced eviction or destitution during this time, leading to an exodus of millions to countries like Canada, the United States, and Australia.

If her family emigrated later, their decision would have been shaped by these hardships. At 3 years old, Emy would have been surrounded by the struggles of her community and may have later carried memories of a changing Ireland or stories passed down from her parents about this pivotal time.

IN 1861, EMY HOBBS was a 19-year-old single woman, Presbyterian by faith, and living in Storrington, Ontario. By this time, she had likely been in Canada for a significant portion of her life, having emigrated from Ireland as a child or young girl. Her Presbyterian faith reflects a common trend among Irish immigrants of Scottish descent or those aligned with Protestantism, which played a significant role in shaping community life and values in Canada West (now Ontario).

As a single young woman in rural Storrington, Emy would likely have been involved in domestic or agricultural work, either helping her family or working in a neighboring household. Social activities centered around the church would have been an important part of her life, offering both spiritual guidance and opportunities for community connections. Emy's presence in Storrington highlights the continuing integration of Irish immigrants into Canadian society, contributing to its growing cultural and demographic fabric.

GENEALOGY ITINERARY:

DAY 1: ARRIVAL IN DUBLIN, Ireland

• Morning: Arrive in Dublin, Ireland. Check into your hotel and rest after your journey.

• Afternoon: Visit the National Library of Ireland to explore genealogical records and gather information about Emy Hobbs' birthplace and early life.

• Evening: Enjoy a traditional Irish dinner at a local pub.

Day 2: Exploring Emy Hobbs' Birthplace

• Morning: Travel to the county where Emy Hobbs was born (e.g., County Offaly or another likely location). Visit local parish churches and cemeteries to find records and graves of the Hobbs family.

• Afternoon: Meet with local historians or genealogists to gain insights into the area during the 1840s.

• Evening: Return to Dublin and relax.

Day 3: Journey to Canada

- Morning: Fly from Dublin to Toronto, Ontario, Canada.

- Afternoon: Drive to Kingston, Ontario, and check into your hotel.

- Evening: Take a leisurely walk around Kingston's historic downtown area.

Day 4: Storrington, Ontario

- Morning: Travel to Storrington, Ontario. Visit the local Presbyterian church where Emy Hobbs was recorded in the 1861 census

Heritage Property INdex » Storrington Township[1]

Explore church records and speak with current church members about its history.

- Afternoon: Visit local cemeteries to find graves of the Hobbs family and pay your respects.

- Evening: Return to Kingston and enjoy dinner at a local restaurant.

Day 5: Kingston and Local Archives

- Morning: Visit the Kingston Frontenac Public Library and the Queen's University Archives to research more about Emy Hobbs' life and family history.

- Afternoon: Explore Kingston's historic sites, such as Fort Henry and the Kingston Penitentiary, to get a sense of the area's history during Emy Hobbs' time.

- Evening: Reflect on your journey and the life of Emy Hobbs over dinner.

Day 6: Departure

---

1. https://ontario.heritagepin.com/storrington-township-in-frontenac/

• Morning: Check out of your hotel and travel back to Toronto.

• Afternoon: Fly back home, carrying with you the memories and discoveries of your genealogical journey.

This itinerary should provide a meaningful and comprehensive way to honor Emy Hobbs' life and legacy.

JOHN M. NEELY

———

J OHN M. NEELY[18]

John M. Neely was born in Upper Canada (present-day Ontario) in 1827, a time of significant development in the region. Upper Canada was experiencing economic and social growth, with settlers working to establish farms, build infrastructure, and develop communities. This was also during the early years of British colonial administration, where laws and governance were being adapted to meet the needs of a rapidly growing settler population.

Life in 1827 would have revolved around agriculture and self-sufficiency, with families relying heavily on the land and natural resources for survival. Education was often informal, though schools were beginning to appear in more established areas. The population was diverse, consisting of Loyalists, immigrants from Britain and Ireland, and Indigenous peoples who played a vital role in the region's history.

John would have grown up amid this frontier-like atmosphere, learning skills essential for life in a rural, developing colony. By the time he reached adulthood, Upper Canada had undergone significant changes, including political reform and the push for responsible government. These developments would have shaped his perspective and opportunities in the decades to come.

———

IN 1839, WHEN PHOTOGRAPHY became publicly available, John M. Neely was 12 years old. The invention of the daguerreotype by Louis Daguerre revolutionized how people captured and preserved memories. Though it would take time for photography to reach rural areas like Upper Canada, the idea of capturing lifelike images instead of relying on paintings or sketches was groundbreaking.

During John's lifetime, the spread of photography would have been a gradual but impactful cultural shift. Early photographers often set up studios in towns and cities, providing portraits for those who could afford them. For people like John, living in Upper Canada, photography might have been seen as an exciting innovation, symbolizing the rapid advancements of the 19th century. However, it likely remained a luxury, with most families only experiencing photography later, during significant life events like weddings or family milestones.

IN 1861, AT 34 YEARS old, John M. Neely was living in Storrington Township, Ontario, as a Presbyterian farmer. At this time, Storrington was a predominantly rural area where farming was the primary livelihood. Farmers like John would have worked hard to maintain their land, growing crops such as wheat, oats, and barley, and raising livestock to sustain their families and contribute to the local economy.

As a Presbyterian, John likely attended regular services and participated in a community centered around faith and moral values. Presbyterianism in Canada was influential during this period, emphasizing education, discipline, and a close-knit congregation. Life in rural Ontario required cooperation with neighbors, with social and religious gatherings being key to building and maintaining relationships within the community.

The census of 1861 also reflects a time of transition in Canada West (now Ontario), with discussions of Confederation gaining traction and innovations like the railroad beginning to reshape rural life. Farmers like John would have been aware of these changes, though their daily routines likely remained focused on the demands of agricultural work.

GENEALOGY ITINERARY:

Day 1: Arrival in Kingston, Ontario

• Morning: Arrive in Kingston, Ontario. Check into your hotel and rest after your journey.

• Afternoon: Visit the Frontenac County Archives to explore birth records and other documents related to John M. Neely's early life in Canada West (now Ontario).

• Evening: Enjoy dinner at a local restaurant in Kingston's historic downtown area.

Day 2: Exploring Storrington, Ontario

• Morning: Travel to Storrington, Ontario. Visit the local Presbyterian church where John M. Neely was recorded in the 1861 census

1861 Canada West (Ontario) - Canada Census[1]

Explore church records and speak with current church members about its history.

• Afternoon: Visit local cemeteries to find graves of the Neely family and pay your respects.

• Evening: Return to Kingston and relax.

Day 3: Kingston and Local Archives

---

1. https://www.geni.com/projects/1861-Canada-West-Ontario-Canada-Census/41183

- Morning: Visit the Kingston Frontenac Public Library and the Queen's University Archives to research more about John M. Neely's life and family history.

- Afternoon: Explore Kingston's historic sites, such as Fort Henry and the Kingston Penitentiary, to get a sense of the area's history during John M. Neely's time.

- Evening: Reflect on your journey and the life of John M. Neely over dinner.

Day 4: Departure

- Morning: Check out of your hotel and travel back to Toronto.

- Afternoon: Fly back home, carrying with you the memories and discoveries of your genealogical journey.

This itinerary should provide a meaningful and comprehensive way to honor John M. Neely's life and legacy.

SARAH T. (UNKNOWN) NEELY

SARAH T. (UNKNOWN) NEELY[19]

Sarah T. Neely, born in Upper Canada in 1839, grew up in a time of significant change and development in the region. Upper Canada was evolving rapidly as settlers expanded communities, built infrastructure, and established institutions to support growing populations.

In the 1830s and 1840s, the area experienced political unrest, including the Upper Canada Rebellion of 1837, which sought more democratic governance. By the time Sarah was born, the Family Compact's influence was waning, and reforms were slowly being implemented. Responsible government would later be established in 1848, shaping the colony's governance.

Growing up in the 1840s and 1850s, Sarah likely witnessed the rise of agriculture as a dominant economic activity in rural areas like Storrington Township, where she would later live. Life for women at this time often revolved around household duties, caring for family members, and contributing to the farm's upkeep. Education for girls was limited but increasingly valued, and literacy rates among settlers were improving.

By 1861, at age 22, Sarah was married to John M. Neely, living as a Presbyterian farmer's wife in Storrington Township. Her role would have included managing domestic responsibilities, possibly assisting with farm work, and participating in the social and religious activities of her community.

ELENOR W. NEELY

<hr>

Elenor W. Neely[20]

Eleanor W. Neely was born in Canada West in 1850, a period of transformation and development in the region that would later become Ontario. During this time, Canada West was thriving as immigration and settlement expanded. Farming communities were growing, and railways were beginning to connect rural areas to larger towns and cities, enhancing trade and communication.

Life for a child like Eleanor in the 1850s would have been centered around family, farm life, and the local community. Education was becoming more accessible, and she may have attended a local schoolhouse, where children typically learned reading, writing, arithmetic, and religious teachings. Presbyterian families like the Neelys often emphasized education and moral instruction.

By 1861, Eleanor, at 11 years old, was living in Storrington Township with her family. She would have likely helped with household and farm tasks, such as tending to younger siblings, fetching water, or assisting with planting and harvesting. Religious practices and Sunday worship would have played a significant role in her upbringing, shaping her values and community connections.

SARAH T. NEELY

S ARAH T. NEELY[21]

Sarah Neely was born in Canada West in 1853, a time when the region was continuing to grow economically and socially. The mid-1850s were marked by the expansion of agriculture, as settlers cleared more land for farming, and the beginnings of industrialization in urban centers. For a family like the Neelys, life would have largely revolved around farming and their Presbyterian faith, which shaped community and family activities.

As a child, Sarah would have experienced a rural upbringing similar to her sister Eleanor's, helping with chores suited to her age and learning skills essential for running a household. Education was becoming increasingly prioritized, so Sarah likely attended a local one-room schoolhouse where she would have been taught basic literacy and numeracy along with religious teachings.

By 1861, at the age of 8, Sarah was living with her family in Storrington Township, likely contributing to daily farm life while also engaging in the tight-knit social and religious community that defined rural life during this era.

MARIAH W. NEELY

MARIAH W. NEELY[22]

Mariah W. Neely was born in Canada West in 1854, during a period of steady development in the region. By this time, agriculture was thriving, supported by improved transportation networks like roads and canals. Families like the Neelys, who were Presbyterian farmers, were part of the backbone of rural communities, relying on hard work and close-knit social and religious ties.

As a young child, Mariah would have grown up in a home where chores were shared among siblings, and religious observance played a significant role in daily life. She would have been surrounded by the sights and sounds of rural farming life, with fields, livestock, and the seasons dictating much of the family's activities.

By 1861, Mariah was 7 years old and living with her family in Storrington Township. Her childhood likely included attending a small local school where she would have learned reading, writing, and arithmetic alongside lessons in Presbyterian doctrine. In the evenings, family prayers and readings from the Bible would have been a central part of the household routine.

JOHN M. NEELY

J OHN M. NEELY[23]

John M. Neely was born in Canada West in 1857, a time when the region was undergoing significant changes as it transitioned from the old colonial structures of Upper Canada to a more settled, prosperous society. By the time he was born, Canada West had seen considerable development in its infrastructure, particularly in transportation and settlement. Many Irish and Scottish immigrants, like his family, had already established themselves in the region, contributing to the rural farming communities.

Growing up in a Presbyterian household, John would have been raised with a strong emphasis on religion and education. His childhood in Storrington would likely have been shaped by the daily rhythms of farm life—working the land, helping with animals, and contributing to the household chores. By 1861, when John was 4 years old, he would have been part of a growing family that was well-integrated into the agricultural economy of the area.

In a community like Storrington, family and church were central pillars of life, with neighbors supporting each other in both social and economic endeavors. Education, too, was important, and John likely attended a local school where he was taught the basics of reading, writing, and arithmetic, in addition to learning about his Presbyterian faith.

SUSAN W. NEELY

S USAN W. NEELY[24]

Susan W. Neely was born in Canada West in 1859, during a time when the region was still experiencing the expansion and development characteristic of the mid-19th century. By the time of her birth, Canada West (now Ontario) had been part of the newly formed Province of Canada since 1841, and the effects of this unification were becoming more apparent. The region had seen an influx of settlers, many of them from Ireland and Scotland, contributing to the agricultural and rural economy.

Growing up in a Presbyterian family in Storrington, Susan would have been part of a close-knit community where religion and family were key to daily life. The early years of her life would have been shaped by a rural lifestyle, with her family likely being involved in farming, a common occupation in the area at the time. Education was valued, so she may have attended the local one-room schoolhouse, where young children were taught reading, writing, arithmetic, and Bible studies.

In 1861, when Susan was around two years old, life in Storrington was simple but hardworking. As with many other families in rural Ontario, her family would have likely been involved in tight-knit community gatherings, church services, and festivals. The sense of community and faith would have formed the foundation of her upbringing.

REV. THOMAS CHAMBERS

RE V. THOMAS CHAMBERS[25]

Thomas Chambers was born in Ireland in 1831, during a period of significant change and challenge in Irish history. Life for most people in Ireland at that time was shaped by rural, agricultural lifestyles and the profound social and economic inequalities that marked the country. Here's what life was like during that era:

Social and Economic Context

Agriculture-Dependent Economy: Ireland's economy was overwhelmingly agrarian. Most of the population lived in the countryside, farming small plots of land. Many tenants relied on the potato as their primary food source, a dependency that would have devastating consequences during the Great Famine (1845-1852).

Tenant Farming: Large estates owned by Anglo-Irish landlords dominated the rural landscape. Farmers often rented small plots of land under unfavorable terms, and evictions were common during difficult times.

Poverty and Inequality: Wealth and power were concentrated in the hands of the Anglo-Irish elite, while the majority of the Irish population lived in poverty, with limited access to education and few opportunities to improve their circumstances.

POLITICAL CLIMATE

Union with Britain: Ireland was part of the United Kingdom of Great Britain and Ireland following the Act of Union in 1801. This led to growing tensions between Irish nationalists, who sought greater independence, and those loyal to British rule.

Catholic Emancipation: The Catholic population, which constituted the majority, had faced severe discrimination for centuries. The Catholic Emancipation Act of 1829 had recently granted Catholics the right to vote and hold political office, leading to a sense of hope but also further political unrest.

CULTURAL AND DAILY Life

Religion: Religion played a central role in Irish life. The Catholic majority often faced social and economic disadvantages, while the Protestant minority, often wealthier and more politically influential, held key positions of power.

Family Life: Families were large, as children were seen as an economic asset to help with farming and household duties. Extended families often lived close to one another, fostering a strong sense of community.

Education: Education for most Irish children was minimal, as schools were scarce in rural areas. However, efforts were underway to establish national schools to provide basic education.

GLOBAL AND TECHNOLOGICAL Advances

Industrial Revolution: While Ireland remained largely agrarian, the Industrial Revolution was transforming parts of Britain. The effects of industrialization in Ireland were limited, leading to a lack of opportunities in urban areas and increased emigration.

Transportation and Communication: The construction of railroads was beginning to link parts of Ireland, making transportation and communication somewhat easier. However, this progress was slow and primarily benefited wealthier areas.

SIGNIFICANCE OF THE Time

Thomas Chambers was born into a society deeply divided by class and religion, on the brink of major upheavals such as the Great Famine and increased emigration. These challenges would have shaped his early years in Ireland, influencing his worldview and possibly motivating his later emigration to Canada, where many sought better opportunities and freedom from the struggles of their homeland.

AT AGE 8, THOMAS CHAMBERS would have experienced the Irish Hurricane of 1839, a devastating and unforgettable storm that struck Ireland on January 6th, 1839. Known as the Night of the Big Wind, it was one of the most severe weather events in Irish history and left a lasting impression on those who lived through it.

What Happened During the Hurricane?

The storm began with an unusually calm and warm winter day, followed by rapidly dropping temperatures and gale-force winds that tore across the country overnight.

The hurricane caused widespread destruction:

Thousands of homes were damaged or destroyed, especially thatched cottages.

Livestock were killed, and crops were flattened, devastating the agrarian economy.

Churches, barns, and trees were uprooted or collapsed under the force of the winds.

PEOPLE WERE TERRIFIED, with some believing it was a sign of divine punishment or an omen of doom.

IMPACT ON DAILY LIFE

For an 8-year-old like Thomas, the hurricane would have been a frightening and formative experience:

Disruption to Family Life: The storm would have likely damaged or destroyed homes and farms, forcing families like his to rebuild from the ground up.

Economic Hardship: Many families, already struggling under tenant farming conditions, faced even greater difficulties as the hurricane wiped out food stores and destroyed tools and property.

Community Resilience: Neighbors likely came together to support one another, as rural communities were tightly knit.

HISTORICAL SIGNIFICANCE

The Night of the Big Wind became a landmark event in Irish collective memory. Decades later, when Ireland introduced old-age pensions in 1909, officials used survivors' memories of the storm as a way to verify their age, as it was such a universally remembered event.

For young Thomas, this hurricane would have been a vivid and possibly traumatic memory that shaped his early experiences in a land already marked by hardship and resilience.

AT 14 YEARS OLD, THOMAS Chambers would have witnessed the beginning of the Great Irish Famine (1845–1852) and the subsequent wave of Irish immigration that defined this era. The year 1845 marked the onset of the potato blight, which devastated Ireland's primary food source, plunging the country into crisis.

The Context of Irish Immigration in 1845

Potato Blight: The fungus Phytophthora infestation spread rapidly across Ireland, destroying potato crops. Since the potato was the staple diet for the majority of the population, its failure led to widespread hunger.

Tenant Farming Pressures: Farmers like Thomas's family often rented small plots of land under exploitative conditions, leaving them vulnerable when crops failed and rents were due.

Mass Emigration: By 1845, families began fleeing Ireland, heading primarily to Canada, the United States, and Australia. This marked the beginning of a massive exodus that would see over a million Irish leave their homeland in the following years.

LIFE FOR A 14-YEAR-Old During Irish Immigration

Economic Hardship: At his age, Thomas would likely have been helping his family on the farm, experiencing firsthand the toll the famine took on agriculture and local communities.

Community Changes: He would have seen neighbors and possibly even family members sell possessions or borrow money for passage to North America. Ships carrying immigrants—later called "coffin ships" for their high death rates—were a common sight in Irish ports.

Emotional Impact: For many young people like Thomas, watching friends and family leave would have been heart-wrenching. Immigration often meant permanent separation.

IMMIGRATION TO CANADA

If Thomas or his family considered immigration, Canada was a popular destination due to its proximity, British ties, and opportunities for farming:

Journey to Canada: Those who immigrated traveled in cramped, unsanitary conditions, leading to outbreaks of disease. Grosse Isle, a quarantine station in Quebec, became infamous for its role during the Irish immigration.

Opportunities Abroad: For those who survived the journey, Canada offered the promise of land and work, though life was still challenging.

FOR A YOUNG BOY LIKE Thomas, 1845 would have been a year of uncertainty, hardship, and dramatic change, as Ireland teetered on the brink of one of its darkest periods. If he emigrated later in life, the memory of this famine and exodus may have played a role in his decision.

IN 1861, THOMAS CHAMBERS was 30 years old, working as a Presbyterian minister, and living in Storrington, Ontario. As a minister, he would have played a central role in the spiritual and social life of his congregation, which often included settlers of Irish or Scottish descent.

Life as a Presbyterian Minister in Storrington, Ontario (1861):

Religious Leadership: Ministers like Thomas were responsible for leading worship services, performing sacraments (such as baptisms, marriages, and funerals), and offering spiritual guidance. Presbyterianism was rooted in Calvinist traditions, emphasizing scripture, education, and moral discipline.

Community Role: Beyond religious duties, Thomas would have acted as a key figure in the community, helping settlers navigate the challenges of rural life in a rapidly developing Canada West. Ministers often mediated disputes, organized charitable efforts, and promoted literacy.

Education and Moral Reform: As education was central to Presbyterian values, Thomas may have been involved in establishing or supporting local schools and promoting Sunday schools to teach both scripture and basic literacy.

Immigrant Settler Communities: Many settlers in the Storrington area were Irish, Scottish, or Ulster-Scots Presbyterians. Thomas likely helped these families adjust to life in a new land, offering spiritual support and community-building activities.

LIVING IN STORRINGTON in 1861:

Storrington was a rural township in Frontenac County, Ontario (then Canada West), characterized by farms, small villages, and a growing population of immigrants and their descendants. Life there involved hard work but also opportunities for growth:

Agricultural Economy: The majority of residents were farmers, raising crops and livestock. The minister often visited parishioners on their farms, providing counsel and support.

Presbyterian Values: The local Presbyterian church would have been a hub of religious and social life, promoting education, sobriety, and community solidarity.

Railway Expansion: By the 1860s, the development of railways was transforming Ontario, connecting rural areas like Storrington to larger markets and cities, which would have influenced the local economy.

AS A 30-YEAR-OLD MINISTER, Thomas Chambers would have been a respected leader in his community, fostering faith, resilience, and social cohesion among his parishioners during a time of significant change in Canada West.

GENEALOGY ITINERARY:

DAY 1: ARRIVAL IN IRELAND

• Morning: Arrive in Dublin, Ireland. Check into your hotel and rest after your journey.

• Afternoon: Visit the National Library of Ireland to explore genealogical records and gather information about Thomas Chambers' birthplace and early life.

• Evening: Enjoy a traditional Irish dinner at a local pub.

Day 2: Exploring Thomas Chambers' Birthplace

• Morning: Travel to the county where Thomas Chambers was born (e.g., Tyrone, Donegal, or Londonderry). Visit local parish churches and cemeteries to find records and graves of the Chambers family.

• Afternoon: Meet with local historians or genealogists to gain insights into the area during the 1830s.

• Evening: Return to Dublin and relax.

Day 3: Journey to Canada

• Morning: Fly from Dublin to Toronto, Ontario, Canada.

• Afternoon: Drive to Kingston, Ontario, and check into your hotel.

• Evening: Take a leisurely walk around Kingston's historic downtown area.

Day 4: Storrington, Ontario

• Morning: Travel to Storrington, Ontario. Visit the local Presbyterian church where Thomas Chambers served as a pastor in 1861. Explore church records and speak with current church members about its history.

• Afternoon: Visit local cemeteries to find Thomas Chambers' grave and pay your respects.

• Evening: Return to Kingston and enjoy dinner at a local restaurant.

Day 5: Kingston and Local Archives

• Morning: Visit the Kingston Frontenac Public Library and the Queen's University Archives to research more about Thomas Chambers' life and work in Ontario.

• Afternoon: Explore Kingston's historic sites, such as Fort Henry and the Kingston Penitentiary, to get a sense of the area's history during Thomas Chambers' time.

• Evening: Reflect on your journey and the life of Thomas Chambers over dinner.

Day 6: Departure

• Morning: Check out of your hotel and travel back to Toronto.

• Afternoon: Fly back home, carrying with you the memories and discoveries of your genealogical journey.

This itinerary should provide a meaningful and comprehensive way to honor Thomas Chambers' life and legacy.

JESSIE D. (UNKNOWN) CHAMBERS

JESSIE D. (UNKNOWN) CHAMBERS[26]

Jessie Chambers was born in Upper Canada in 1834, a time when the region was experiencing significant growth, political tension, and early settlement expansion.

Life in Upper Canada in 1834

Growing Communities: By 1834, Upper Canada (modern-day Ontario) was seeing an influx of settlers, particularly from Britain, Ireland, and the United States. Small towns were growing, and Toronto (then York) officially became a city in 1834.

Agriculture and Settlement: The economy was largely agricultural, with settlers clearing land, building homesteads, and farming crops like wheat, oats, and barley. Life was physically demanding, especially for women, who played essential roles in managing households, raising children, and contributing to farm work.

Social Structure: Society was hierarchical, with landowners, professionals, and clergy enjoying higher status. Many settlers were religious, and church communities provided spiritual and social cohesion. Presbyterians were particularly prominent among Scottish and Ulster-Scots settlers.

Political Context: This period preceded the Rebellions of 1837, as discontent with the oligarchic rule of the "Family Compact" was already simmering. Reformers pushed for greater representation and democracy in Upper Canada.

JESSIE'S EARLY LIFE

Growing up in Upper Canada, Jessie would have experienced the challenges of rural settlement:

Education opportunities were limited, often provided by churches or informal local schools.

Her upbringing likely included household duties, such as sewing, cooking, childcare, and supporting the family's farm or trade.

Religious faith would have been a cornerstone of her upbringing, especially if she was part of a Presbyterian family.

———

JESSIE CHAMBERS WAS 6 years old in 1841 when Upper Canada and Lower Canada were united into the Province of Canada under the Act of Union.

The Act of Union, 1841

This act merged Upper Canada (modern-day Ontario) and Lower Canada (modern-day Quebec) into a single political entity called the Province of Canada.

It was intended to create political stability after the Rebellions of 1837-1838 and address economic challenges.

The new Province was divided into Canada West (formerly Upper Canada) and Canada East (formerly Lower Canada), with a single legislature in Kingston, the first capital of the united Province.

———

LIFE FOR A 6-YEAR-OLD in 1841

At 6 years old, Jessie's world would have revolved around family, community, and daily chores:

Education: Limited schooling would have been available, often through small church-run schools where children learned reading, writing, and arithmetic.

Daily Life: Jessie likely helped with small household tasks such as tidying, feeding animals, or learning domestic skills like sewing and cooking.

Rural Life: For families in Upper Canada, survival required cooperation. Farming families worked long days, with children playing a role early in life.

Community and Church: Religion was a strong influence, and families attended church regularly. The Presbyterian faith likely guided much of Jessie's upbringing.

THE UNIFICATION OF the Canadas marked the beginning of new political and economic changes, but for young children like Jessie, the day-to-day challenges of life in early 19th-century Upper Canada remained constant.

JESSIE CHAMBERS WAS 13 years old in 1848 when the Principle of Responsible Government was established in the Province of Canada.

The Principle of Responsible Government (1848):

This principle marked a shift in colonial governance, giving elected representatives control over the government, rather than appointed officials or colonial governors.

The governor would now act on the advice of an Executive Council that was accountable to the elected assembly.

This development was largely driven by Lord Elgin (Governor General) and reform leaders like Robert Baldwin and Louis-Hippolyte LaFontaine.

IMPACT ON LIFE IN UPPER Canada (Canada West):

For Jessie and her family, the establishment of responsible government was significant politically, but the immediate changes in daily life would have been subtle:

Community Engagement: It gave communities more faith in local representatives and contributed to a growing Canadian identity.

Economy: The improved governance encouraged infrastructure development, agriculture, and trade, which would benefit rural families.

Presbyterian Influence: As part of a Presbyterian household, Jessie's family likely supported principles of reform and moral governance that aligned with responsible government ideals.

AT 13 YEARS OLD, JESSIE would have been old enough to overhear discussions about these political changes, particularly in church or community gatherings, while continuing her day-to-day responsibilities at home in Upper Canada.

BY THE TIME JESSIE married Thomas Chambers and became the wife of a Presbyterian minister, she would have been well-prepared for the responsibilities of supporting her husband's work. Ministerial wives were expected to assist with church activities, organize charitable efforts, and host community gatherings, all while managing their own households. In 1861, Jessie Chambers, at 27 years old, would have been integral to both her husband's ministry and the social fabric of Storrington, Ontario.

ELLA JANE CHAMBERS

E LLA JANE CHAMBERS[27]

Ella Jane Chambers was born in Picton, Canada West in 1857.

What was life like in Canada West (1857)?

Economy: The 1850s were a period of growth and development in Canada West. Agricultural practices were improving, and many towns, including Picton, were flourishing due to farming, trade, and emerging industries like mills and shipbuilding.

Picton: Located in Prince Edward County, Picton was a bustling port town along the Bay of Quinte, known for its active harbor, lumber trade, and farming economy. By 1857, it would have been a growing community with schools, churches, and local markets.

Transportation: The Grand Trunk Railway had been expanding across Canada West, improving travel and trade, though Picton was still primarily reliant on water routes and horse-drawn transport.

Religion: As the daughter of a Presbyterian minister, Ella Jane would have been raised in a deeply religious household where church life played a central role in both worship and community events.

Daily Life: Ella Jane's early years would have been filled with typical rural activities—family chores, schooling, and church attendance—alongside the social life of a close-knit Presbyterian community.

IN 1857, PICTON WAS becoming an established town, offering Ella Jane's family stability, opportunities, and a growing sense of identity within the developing colony of Canada West.

IN 1861, 4-YEAR-OLD Ella Jane Chambers was living in Storrington, Ontario as the daughter of a Presbyterian minister, Thomas Chambers, and his wife, Jessie.

Life as a Pastor's Daughter in 1861:

Religious Environment: Ella Jane's life would have revolved around the church and its community. As the child of a pastor, she likely attended church regularly, surrounded by hymns, sermons, and Sunday school teachings.

Family Role: Pastor's families often played key roles in their congregation. Jessie, her mother, likely assisted in organizing church events and hosting gatherings, while young Ella Jane would have been raised with expectations of good behavior and manners.

Community Respect: As part of a minister's family, Ella Jane would have been well-known and respected in the local community, with her father seen as a moral and spiritual leader.

Daily Life: At 4 years old, Ella Jane's days would have been filled with simple household chores, learning her ABCs, and playing with siblings or neighboring children in the rural landscape of Storrington.

Rural Storrington: The family lived in a small, close-knit community where farming was the main livelihood. Life would have been simple but full of activity, with a mix of hard work, church gatherings, and seasonal events.

AS THE DAUGHTER OF a minister in 1861 Ontario, Ella Jane's upbringing was shaped by faith, community, and the modest comforts of a rural Canadian life.

JESSIE CHAMBERS

JESSIE CHAMBERS[28]

Jessie Chambers was born on July 1, 1858, in Canada West, during a time of significant change and growth in the region.

Life in Canada West in 1858:

Canada West: Formerly Upper Canada, it was part of the united Province of Canada (formed in 1841). By 1858, Canada West was experiencing population growth, economic development, and increasing political discussions about Confederation.

Family Life: As part of a pastor's family, Jessie would have been born into a household where faith, community service, and education were prioritized. Her father, Thomas Chambers, as a Presbyterian minister, likely led a life dedicated to the spiritual and social well-being of his congregation.

Daily Living: The Chambers family's rural lifestyle would have involved simplicity and self-sufficiency, with Jessie growing up surrounded by farm life, church gatherings, and community support.

Milestone Birthdate: Jessie's birth coincided with a period when Canada West was emerging as a key player in discussions about Canada's political future, a few years before Confederation in 1867.

IN 1861:

By 1861, Jessie was 2 years old, living in Storrington, Ontario, as part of her father's household. She would have been cared for by her mother, Jessie Chambers (Sr.), alongside her older sister, Ella Jane, in a household shaped by faith, family, and rural Canadian life.

EMILY CHAMBERS

E MILY CHAMBERS[29]

Emily Chambers was born in Canada West in 1859, a period when the region was experiencing rapid development and social transformation.

Life in Canada West in 1859:

Canada West: Formerly Upper Canada, the region was part of the united Province of Canada. The economy was growing with agriculture as the backbone, and cities like Toronto and Hamilton were expanding.

Technological Progress: The railway boom was well underway, improving transportation for goods and people. Innovations such as telegraphs were beginning to connect communities.

Family and Faith: As the daughter of a Presbyterian minister, Emily would have been born into a devout household where faith, education, and community service were central to daily life. Church gatherings and Sunday schools would have been central activities.

Home Life: Life in a rural community like Storrington emphasized simplicity, with a strong reliance on farming, family bonds, and local support systems.

BY 1861:

In 1861, Emily was 2 years old, living with her family in Storrington, Ontario. As the youngest child at the time, she would have been cared for primarily by her mother, Jessie Chambers (Sr.), alongside her older sisters, Ella Jane (4 years old) and Jessie (3 years old). Her father's role as a minister meant the family was likely well-respected and closely tied to the local Presbyterian community.

ELISABETH CHAMBERS

E LISABETH CHAMBERS[30]

Elisabeth Chambers was born in Canada West in 1860, during a time of continued growth and societal transformation in the Province of Canada.

Life in Canada West in 1860:

Economic Growth: Canada West's economy remained strongly agricultural, but urban centers were expanding, with improved transportation through railways and canals bolstering trade and migration.

Social Values: Family and church life were the cornerstones of society, especially for the children of clergy like Elisabeth's father, Thomas Chambers, a Presbyterian minister. Religion played a central role in community and education.

Daily Life: The Chambers household would have been guided by Presbyterian values, with a focus on morality, education, and service. Elisabeth's mother, Jessie Chambers, likely managed a busy household while raising her growing family.

BY 1861:

In 1861, Elisabeth was 1 year old and living in Storrington, Ontario, the youngest child in a family with four older sisters:

Ella Jane (4)

Jessie (3)

Emily (2)

––––––––––––––––––––

AS THE DAUGHTER OF a pastor, Elisabeth's early years would have been spent in a home deeply connected to the church and community life, surrounded by the sounds of sermons, hymns, and family prayer.

GEORGE NOBBS

G EORGE NOBBS[31]

George Nobbs was born in England in 1821, a time of significant transformation in Britain.

Life in England in 1821:

The Industrial Revolution: By the 1820s, England was rapidly transitioning from an agrarian economy to an industrial powerhouse. Factories, mills, and coal mines were booming, changing the landscape of cities and towns.

Population Growth: England's population was steadily increasing due to improvements in sanitation, medicine, and agricultural productivity, although many still lived in poverty.

Social Order: The rigid class system shaped opportunities and daily life. The working class toiled in harsh conditions, while the upper and middle classes prospered.

Regency Era: Culturally, this was the tail end of the Regency period (1811-1820), with King George IV beginning his reign in 1820. Literature, architecture, and fashion flourished during this era.

Emigration: Economic hardships and social change prompted many to leave England for the colonies, seeking land, opportunity, and a better life.

GEORGE NOBBS WAS BORN into a world on the cusp of massive technological and societal advancements, and his decision to eventually settle in Canada reflects the broader trend of emigration from England during the 19th century.

———

AT THE AGE OF 2, IN 1823, the sport of rugby was said to have been invented. According to popular legend, during a game of football (soccer) at Rugby School in England, a student named William Webb Ellis picked up the ball and ran with it. This unconventional act laid the foundation for what would become rugby football.

Though the story is somewhat romanticized, it reflects the growing trend of formalizing and codifying sports in early 19th-century England. Schools and universities were central to these efforts, leading to the creation of organized games that emphasized discipline, teamwork, and competition—values that resonated with England's evolving industrial and imperial identity.

For George Nobbs, this period was part of a rapidly modernizing England, where even leisure activities were being transformed into structured pursuits that would spread worldwide through British influence.

———

AT THE AGE OF 18, IN 1839, photography became publicly available with the announcement of the daguerreotype process by Louis Daguerre in France. This revolutionary method was the first practical photographic technique, allowing for detailed and permanent images. Around the same time, William Henry Fox Talbot in England developed the calotype process, which used negatives to produce multiple prints.

For George Nobbs, living in early Victorian England, the emergence of photography marked a significant moment in history. It captured a rapidly changing society, from industrial progress to personal milestones, and began democratizing visual representation. Photography's introduction must have seemed nothing short of magic—an innovation that allowed ordinary people to preserve their likenesses and moments in a way never before possible.

AT 22 YEARS OLD, IN 1843, A Christmas Carol by Charles Dickens was published. The novella quickly became a beloved holiday classic, capturing the social and economic struggles of Victorian England through the redemption story of Ebenezer Scrooge. Dickens' work highlighted the harsh realities of poverty and the importance of compassion, themes that resonated deeply with the public.

For George Nobbs, living in England during this period, A Christmas Carol would have reflected the contrasts of his time—industrial progress alongside widespread inequality. The story's emphasis on charity, family, and goodwill mirrored the growing Victorian focus on morality and social reform, especially as Christmas became a more celebrated and family-centered holiday.

IN 1861, AT 40 YEARS old, George Nobbs was an Anglican blacksmith living in Storrington, Ontario. As a blacksmith, he played a vital role in the community, crafting and repairing tools, horseshoes, farming equipment, and more. Blacksmiths were essential to rural life in Upper Canada, supporting both agriculture and transportation.

By this time, Storrington was part of Canada West (formerly Upper Canada), where settlements were growing, and industries like farming and logging flourished. Anglicanism was prominent among English immigrants, and George would have likely attended regular services in a local parish, forming part of the close-knit community that leaned heavily on faith, family, and hard work.

Life as a blacksmith was labor-intensive. The trade demanded skill, strength, and precision. George's shop would have been a hub of activity, with farmers, travelers, and neighbors relying on his expertise to keep their equipment and tools in working order. In the growing settlements of the 1860s, blacksmithing was a steady and respected profession.

GENEALOGY ITINERARY:

DAY 1: ARRIVAL AND Initial Research

• Morning: Arrive in Storrington, Ontario.

• Afternoon: Visit the local library or archives to gather any available records on George Nobbs. Look for census records, land deeds, and any local history books that might mention him.

• Evening: Review the collected information and plan the next day's visits.

Day 2: Exploring Storrington

• Morning: Visit the Anglican church in Storrington. Check church records for any mentions of George Nobbs, such as baptism, marriage, or burial records.

• Afternoon: Visit the local cemetery to find George Nobbs' grave. Take photos and note any inscriptions.

• Evening: Visit the local historical society or museum to learn more about the life of blacksmiths in the 1860s.

Day 3: Broader Research and Exploration

• Morning: Travel to nearby towns or cities where additional records might be held, such as Kingston, Ontario. Visit archives or libraries there.

• Afternoon: Visit any relevant historical sites or museums that could provide context about the era and lifestyle of George Nobbs.

• Evening: Compile all gathered information and start building a detailed family tree.

Day 4: Final Research and Wrap-Up

• Morning: Revisit any locations for follow-up research or to gather additional details.

• Afternoon: Organize all documents, photos, and notes. Create a digital backup of all collected information.

• Evening: Reflect on the trip and plan any future research steps.

Tips for a Successful Genealogy Trip

1. Prepare in Advance: Make a list of all the places you want to visit and the records you hope to find

How to Plan a Successful Genealogy Road Trip | Amy Johnson Crow[1]

2. Stay Organized: Keep a detailed log of all your findings and where you found them.

3. Be Flexible: Sometimes unexpected discoveries can lead to new and exciting information.

---

1. https://www.amyjohnsoncrow.com/genealogy-road-trip/

4. Engage with Locals: Talk to local historians or long-time residents who might have additional insights.

DEBRY (UNKNOWN) NOBBS

DEBRY (UNKNOWN) NOBBS[32]

Debry Nobbs was born in 1817 in Ireland, a time marked by British control and significant socio-economic struggles for the Irish population. The early 19th century in Ireland was characterized by poverty, agrarian unrest, and class divisions, with most of the population living in rural areas and working as tenant farmers under British landlords.

By the time Debry was born, Ireland was beginning to feel the economic pressures that would eventually culminate in the Great Famine of the 1840s. Her childhood would likely have been influenced by a subsistence lifestyle, with strong familial and community bonds offering support in difficult times. Religion also played a central role in Irish life, with tensions often present between Catholic and Protestant communities, depending on her family's faith.

When Debry immigrated to Canada—likely during or after the famine years—she would have encountered a fresh start in Canada West, which promised greater opportunity for land, work, and stability.

DEBRY NOBBS WAS 28 years old when the Irish immigration wave began in 1845, driven by the devastating effects of the Great Famine. This period saw a massive exodus of Irish people fleeing starvation, disease, and poverty, with many arriving in Canada seeking refuge and a chance at a better life.

At this age, Debry may have already been married or contemplating her own future as the famine intensified. If she immigrated around this time, she would have faced the harrowing conditions aboard "coffin ships" and the challenges of resettling in a foreign land. Her experiences during this tumultuous period likely shaped her resilience and determination as she built a new life in Canada West. By 1861, she had established herself in Storrington, Ontario, alongside her husband, George Nobbs, contributing to their household and community.

BY 1861, AT 44 YEARS old, Debry was living with her husband, George Nobbs, in Storrington, Ontario. As the wife of a blacksmith, her role would have been vital in supporting her household, managing domestic duties, and possibly contributing to their livelihood by taking care of customers or bookkeeping. Women like Debry were the backbone of rural communities, ensuring that families thrived amid the hardships of pioneer life.

CARLINE NOBBS

CARLINE NOBBS[33]

Carline Nobbs was born in Canada West in 1845, a time marked by significant immigration to the region, particularly from Ireland and Britain. This was the same year the Great Irish Famine began, prompting many Irish families to leave their homeland in search of better opportunities in North America, including Canada.

In Canada West, life would have been both challenging and full of opportunity for settlers like Carline's family. The land was being settled and cleared for farming, and towns and villages were developing. The region saw growing infrastructure, such as roads, schools, and churches, to accommodate the increasing population. Carline, born to an English blacksmith father and an Irish mother, likely grew up in a hardworking household that balanced her father's trade with the demands of pioneer life.

CARLINE NOBBS WAS 1 year old in 1846 when the sewing machine was patented. This invention, patented by Elias Howe, revolutionized the textile industry and domestic life. Before the sewing machine, all sewing had to be done by hand, a time-consuming and labor-intensive task. The machine eventually allowed for faster, more efficient clothing production and eased some of the burdens of household sewing, particularly for women in pioneer families like Carline's.

Though sewing machines were not yet common in households during her childhood, their eventual spread in the mid-19th century symbolized a turning point in domestic labor and craftsmanship. For Carline's family in Canada West, her mother, Debry, likely still relied on hand sewing in the 1840s, mending clothes and producing garments as part of the daily rhythm of life in rural Storrington.

BY 1861, CARLINE WOULD have been 16 years old, living with her family in Storrington, Ontario, during a period when rural communities were still closely tied to agriculture and trades. Anglican, like her father, she likely attended local church services and helped with family responsibilities while preparing for her own adult life in this evolving society.

THOMAS NOBBS

THOMAS NOBBS[34]

Thomas Nobbs was born in Canada West in 1848, a time when rural Upper Canada was experiencing steady development and transformation. Families like the Nobbs were contributing to the growth of small farming and trade communities, such as those in Storrington Township.

In 1848:

The population in Canada West continued to rise, bolstered by British and Irish immigrants escaping economic hardship or seeking better opportunities.

Small towns and rural areas relied heavily on skilled tradesmen, like blacksmiths (such as Thomas's father, George Nobbs), to maintain tools, wagons, and agricultural equipment.

Schools were improving, though many rural children, particularly boys, were often needed on farms or in trades by their teenage years.

THOMAS WOULD HAVE GROWN up surrounded by the hard work of frontier life, in a family balancing their trade with the demands of rural living. As the second half of the 19th century unfolded, his generation would witness significant changes, including improved infrastructure, railways, and further agricultural mechanization.

GRACE NOBBS

G RACE NOBBS[35]

Grace Nobbs was born in Canada West in 1855, a time when rural communities like Storrington Township were becoming more established and closely tied to agriculture and trade.

In 1855:

Canada West (modern-day Ontario) was part of the Province of Canada, and the population was growing due to continued immigration from Britain and Ireland.

Life in rural areas centered on family, church, and community. Anglican families like the Nobbs often attended services regularly, with religion playing a central role in daily life.

For young girls like Grace, childhood likely included helping with household chores, tending to siblings, and attending school if one was accessible nearby. Education for girls was becoming more common, but their primary focus was still preparation for future roles as homemakers.

GRACE GREW UP IN A family environment shaped by her father's trade as a blacksmith, giving her an early understanding of the importance of hard work and self-reliance in building a prosperous life.

GEORGE HOWES

G EORGE HOWES[36]

George Howes was born in England in 1816, during the Regency era, a time marked by social stratification, industrial progress, and significant global events.

Life in 1816:

The Year Without a Summer: A volcanic eruption in 1815 caused climate abnormalities, leading to failed crops and food shortages in parts of Europe, including England.

Industrial Revolution: England was the heart of the Industrial Revolution, with rapid developments in textiles, steam power, and transportation. However, rural areas still relied heavily on traditional farming.

Social Structure: Class distinctions were deeply entrenched. A working-class family like George's would likely have faced long hours of labor with limited opportunities for upward mobility.

Literature and Arts: This was also the era of Jane Austen's novels, reflecting the manners and societal structures of the time.

GROWING UP DURING THIS transformative period, George would have witnessed both the challenges of rural life and the technological advancements shaping the world. His later decision to emigrate to Canada likely reflects the lure of new opportunities in a rapidly expanding colony.

AT 7 YEARS OLD IN 1823, George Howes was living in England when rugby was invented. Legend has it that William Webb Ellis, a student at Rugby School, picked up the ball during a game of football (soccer) and ran with it, creating the foundations of rugby football.

While the game was initially confined to schools and local clubs, it symbolized a growing culture of organized sports during the 19th century, which emphasized teamwork, discipline, and physical endurance—values that would shape communities and societies in the Victorian era. If George had been exposed to news or discussions about sports, rugby might have been a topic of curiosity or pride as a uniquely English invention.

AT 27 YEARS OLD IN 1843, George Howes was living in England when Charles Dickens published A Christmas Carol. This novella quickly became a holiday classic and reflected the social and economic realities of Victorian England. It highlighted themes of charity, redemption, and the plight of the working class, resonating deeply with the challenges many faced during the Industrial Revolution.

For George, living in this era meant witnessing a society grappling with rapid urbanization, class divides, and changing attitudes towards poverty and philanthropy. The book's release would have been a significant cultural event, possibly discussed in local communities, newspapers, and gatherings, as it spoke to the heart of societal transformation in 19th-century England.

AT 30 YEARS OLD IN 1846, George Howes witnessed the patenting of the sewing machine by Elias Howe. This invention revolutionized textile production and tailoring, greatly reducing the time and labor needed to produce garments.

For someone like George, living in the mid-19th century, the sewing machine symbolized the growing influence of mechanization on everyday life and industries. Its introduction marked a shift in how clothing was made, transitioning from handmade to machine-assisted production, and would have had a profound impact on households and the economy. It was a time of rapid technological advancement, laying the foundation for the industrialized future.

IN 1861, GEORGE HOWES, a 45-year-old laborer and Anglican, was living in Storrington, Ontario. At this time, Storrington was a rural township where agriculture and manual labor were integral to the local economy. As a laborer, George likely worked in physically demanding roles, possibly assisting with farming, construction, or other essential tasks that supported the community's growth.

His Anglican faith would have connected him to the established Church of England, which played a significant role in providing spiritual guidance and fostering a sense of community in Upper Canada. The Anglican church often held social gatherings, which were an important aspect of life in these small, tight-knit communities. Living in Ontario during this period also meant experiencing the ongoing transformation brought by advancements in transportation, such as the expansion of railroads, and changes in agriculture and industry.

GENEALOGY ITINERARY:

Day 1: Arrival in England

• Morning: Arrive in London, England. Check into your hotel and rest after your flight.

• Afternoon: Visit the British Library to explore genealogical records and historical documents that might provide more information about George Howes' early life.

• Evening: Enjoy a traditional English dinner at a local pub.

Day 2: Gloucestershire, England

• Morning: Travel to Gloucestershire, where George Howes was born in 1816

https://www.findmypast.co.uk/1881-census/
george-howes-0011540355

Visit local archives and libraries to search for birth records and other relevant documents.

• Afternoon: Explore the Gloucestershire Archives and the Gloucester Cathedral, which might have historical records of baptisms and other church activities.

• Evening: Stay overnight in a charming bed and breakfast in Gloucestershire.

Day 3: Historical Sites in England

• Morning: Visit West Winch, Norfolk, where George Howes was an agricultural labourer according to the 1841 and 1851 census

A Skeleton in the Closet by Ellen Maki, Ph.D.[1]

Explore local historical sites and cemeteries.

---

1. https://findingfolk.org/2016/06/a-family-neer-do-well-in-the-news/

- Afternoon: Head back to London and prepare for your flight to Canada.

- Evening: Fly to Toronto, Ontario.

Day 4: Arrival in Ontario, Canada

- Morning: Arrive in Toronto and drive to Storrington, Ontario.

- Afternoon: Check into your accommodation in Storrington. Visit the Storrington and District Museum to learn about the local history and George Howes' life as a labourer in the 1860s

The Storrington and District Museum - Times Past[2]

- EVENING: RELAX AND enjoy the scenic views of the Rideau Lakes area.

Day 5: Exploring Storrington

- Morning: Visit local churches in Storrington, such as the Anglican Church, to find baptism, marriage, and burial records.

- Afternoon: Explore the Heritage Property Index for Storrington Township to find historical sites and land records

Heritage Property INdex » Storrington Township[3]

- EVENING: ENJOY A peaceful evening by the lake.

Day 6: Kingston, Ontario

2. http://www.storringtonmuseum.org/the_collection/times_past/

3. https://ontario.heritagepin.com/storrington-township-in-frontenac/

- Morning: Drive to Kingston, Ontario. Visit the Shoal Tower National Historic Site and the Kingston Association of Museums, Art Galleries & Historic Sites

https://parks.canada.ca/lhn-nhs/on/kingston/shoal-tower[4]

https://www.kingstonmuseums.ca/about/contact-us[5]

- AFTERNOON: EXPLORE the 1000 Islands History Museum in Gananoque to learn more about the region's history

1000 Islands History Museum[6]

- EVENING: RETURN TO Storrington for your final night.

Day 7: Departure

- Morning: Spend your last morning in Storrington, perhaps revisiting any sites of interest or conducting final research.

- Afternoon: Drive back to Toronto for your flight home.

- Evening: Depart from Toronto, concluding your genealogical journey.

I hope this itinerary helps you connect with George Howes' past and uncover more about his life and heritage!

---

4. https://parks.canada.ca/lhn-nhs/on/kingston/shoal-towerhttps://www.kingstonmuseums.ca/about/contact-us

5. https://parks.canada.ca/lhn-nhs/on/kingston/shoal-towerhttps://www.kingstonmuseums.ca/about/contact-us

6. https://www.1000islandshistorymuseum.com/

ANNE (UNKNOWN) HOWES

A NNE (UNKNOWN) HOWES[37]

Anne Howes, born in 1819 in Ireland, lived through significant events before settling in Storrington, Ontario with her husband, George. Her early years in Ireland would have been shaped by the political unrest and hardships of the early 19th century, including the Irish Rebellion of 1798's aftermath and ongoing tensions between Ireland and Britain.

By the time Anne immigrated to Canada, likely in the mid-1800s, many Irish families were seeking better opportunities due to poverty and limited prospects at home. As an Anglican, her faith would have played a key role in her transition, connecting her with others of similar backgrounds in her new community.

ANNE HOWES WAS 7 YEARS old in 1826 when matches were invented by John Walker in England. This innovation was revolutionary for its time, making fire-starting much more convenient than previous methods like flint and steel. While living in Ireland, Anne's family may not have had immediate access to this invention, as new technologies often took time to spread, especially to rural areas. However, it marked the beginning of significant advancements in daily life that Anne would witness throughout her lifetime.

ANNE HOWES WAS 26 YEARS old during the Irish immigration of 1845, which marked the beginning of the Great Famine. This tragic period saw a mass exodus of Irish people fleeing starvation and poverty, many of them emigrating to North America. Although Anne was already an adult, the famine and its aftermath likely shaped her views and experiences, particularly if she emigrated around this time. The influx of Irish immigrants to Canada West (modern Ontario) would have contributed to the communities where Anne eventually settled.

IN 1861, ANNE WAS 42 years old, married to George, and living in Storrington, Ontario. Women in rural communities often contributed to the family by managing the household, raising children, and assisting with tasks like gardening, food preservation, or even helping with labor-intensive farm work. Life would have required resilience and adaptability, especially given her Irish roots and the challenges of immigration and settlement.

THOMAS SHANNON

T HOMAS SHANNON[38]

Thomas Shannon was born in Ireland in 1815, a time when Ireland was predominantly rural and agrarian, with most of the population relying on agriculture for their livelihood. The country was under British rule, and economic and social inequality was widespread. Tenant farming was common, and many Irish families lived in poverty, struggling to pay rents to absentee landlords.

This period saw the early stirrings of industrialization in some parts of Ireland, but for the majority, life remained centered around subsistence farming. Political tensions were high, with movements advocating for Catholic emancipation and Irish self-governance beginning to gain momentum. The Napoleonic Wars had ended the year before, in 1814, bringing economic challenges as wartime demands ceased.

Thomas would have grown up witnessing these struggles, and like many of his generation, may have chosen to emigrate in search of better opportunities, eventually settling in Canada.

THOMAS SHANNON WAS 2 years old when the first prototype of the bicycle, the Draisine or "running machine," was invented in 1817 by Karl Drais in Germany. This invention was a precursor to the modern bicycle and marked the beginning of a new era in personal transportation. However, it would take several decades before bicycles became widely used and accessible.

THOMAS SHANNON WAS 11 years old in 1826 when John Walker, an English chemist, invented the first friction matches. These matches used a mixture of antimony sulfide and potassium chlorate, igniting when struck on a rough surface. This innovation was a significant step forward in making fire-starting more convenient and portable, changing daily life for people worldwide.

THOMAS SHANNON WAS 24 years old in 1839 when the Irish Hurricane struck. This devastating storm caused widespread destruction along Ireland's west coast, destroying homes, crops, and infrastructure. It was one of the most severe weather events of the 19th century in Ireland, leading to significant hardships, especially for the rural poor who depended on agriculture. The storm's aftermath likely intensified economic struggles, adding to the factors driving Irish emigration during that era.

IN 1861, THOMAS SHANNON was 46 years old, Anglican, and living in Storrington, Ontario. As a settler in Storrington Township, he would have been part of a rural farming community, working to establish a stable livelihood. The Anglican Church played a significant role in the lives of settlers, serving as both a religious and social center.

Life at this time was centered around agriculture, with settlers striving to clear land, grow crops, and care for livestock. The community likely consisted of fellow Irish immigrants and others from the British Isles, creating a network of shared experiences and mutual support. The challenges of farming in the Canadian wilderness, including harsh winters and limited infrastructure, would have been balanced by the growing opportunities in the Province of Canada, which was on the cusp of Confederation in 1867.

GENEALOGY ITINERARY:

Day 1: Arrival in Ireland

• Morning: Arrive in Dublin, Ireland. Check into your hotel and rest after your flight.

• Afternoon: Visit the National Library of Ireland to explore genealogical records and historical documents that might provide more information about Thomas Shannon's early life.

• Evening: Enjoy a traditional Irish dinner at a local pub.

Day 2: County Cork, Ireland

• Morning: Travel to County Cork, where many Shannons were historically located

Cork Genealogy Online Search facility, Mallow North and East – Roots Ireland[1]

Visit local archives and libraries to search for birth records and other relevant documents.

• Afternoon: Explore the Cork City and County Archives and the St. Fin Barre's Cathedral, which might have historical records of baptisms and other church activities.

• Evening: Stay overnight in a charming bed and breakfast in Cork.

Day 3: Historical Sites in Ireland

• Morning: Visit local parishes in County Cork to find more detailed records of Thomas Shannon's family.

---

1. https://www.rootsireland.ie/cork-genealogy/cork-online-sources/

- Afternoon: Head back to Dublin and prepare for your flight to Canada.

- Evening: Fly to Toronto, Ontario.

Day 4: Arrival in Ontario, Canada

- Morning: Arrive in Toronto and drive to Storrington, Ontario.

- Afternoon: Check into your accommodation in Storrington. Visit the Storrington and District Museum to learn about the local history and Thomas Shannon's life as an Anglican in the 1860s

The Storrington and District Museum - Times Past[2]

- EVENING: RELAX AND enjoy the scenic views of the Rideau Lakes area.

Day 5: Exploring Storrington

- Morning: Visit local churches in Storrington, such as the Anglican Church, to find baptism, marriage, and burial records.

- Afternoon: Explore the Heritage Property Index for Storrington Township to find historical sites and land records

Heritage Property INdex » Storrington Township[3]

- EVENING: ENJOY A peaceful evening by the lake.

Day 6: Kingston, Ontario

----

2. http://www.storringtonmuseum.org/the_collection/times_past/

3. https://ontario.heritagepin.com/storrington-township-in-frontenac/

- Morning: Drive to Kingston, Ontario. Visit the Shoal Tower National Historic Site and the Kingston Association of Museums, Art Galleries & Historic Sites

City Hall | City of Kingston[4]

https://www.forthenry.com/

- AFTERNOON: EXPLORE the 1000 Islands History Museum in Gananoque to learn more about the region's history

1000 Islands History Museum[5]

- EVENING: RETURN TO Storrington for your final night.

Day 7: Departure

- Morning: Spend your last morning in Storrington, perhaps revisiting any sites of interest or conducting final research.

- Afternoon: Drive back to Toronto for your flight home.

- Evening: Depart from Toronto, concluding your genealogical journey.

I hope this itinerary helps you connect with Thomas Shannon's past and uncover more about his life and heritage!

EDWARD SHANNON

---

4. https://www.cityofkingston.ca/arts-culture-and-events/history-and-heritage/city-hall/

5. https://www.1000islandshistorymuseum.com/

EDWARD SHANNON[39]

Edward Shannon was born in Ireland in 1849, a time of great hardship during the Irish Famine (1845–1852). His early years would have been shaped by the effects of widespread poverty, emigration, and social upheaval caused by the famine. Many Irish families were forced to leave their homeland during this period, seeking better opportunities abroad, particularly in Canada, the United States, and Australia.

IN 1861, EDWARD SHANNON was 12 years old, Anglican, and living in Storrington, Ontario. At this age, he would likely have been helping his family with daily tasks, possibly on a farm or in another labor-intensive environment. Education may have been limited, with school attendance dependent on the family's resources and priorities.

Living in Storrington, a rural township in Canada West (modern-day Ontario), Edward would have experienced life in a close-knit community shaped by agriculture and the Anglican Church, which played a central role in social and spiritual life. The area would have been marked by the hard work of pioneering families and the blending of immigrant cultures. Edward's Irish roots may have influenced his family's traditions, though they were integrating into the fabric of Upper Canadian society.

SIMEON SPOONER

SIMEON SPOONER[40]

Simeon Spooner, born in Châteauguay, Quebec, in 1802, came into the world during an era when Lower Canada (modern-day Quebec) was transitioning from its French colonial past to being part of British North America. Châteauguay, a small town located near the St. Lawrence River, was a largely agricultural community.

During this time, the population of Lower Canada was mostly rural, with farming being the predominant occupation. The region was heavily influenced by its French Catholic majority, though British influences were increasingly felt following the British conquest of New France in 1763.

In 1802, Châteauguay would have been relatively peaceful, but political tensions between English and French-speaking residents would grow over the following decades. Simeon's early life likely involved a mix of farming and navigating a bilingual and bicultural society. By the War of 1812, when Simeon was about 10, Châteauguay would play a critical role, as it was the site of a major battle in 1813.

SIMEON SPOONER WAS 5 years old when slavery was abolished in the British colonies in 1807. While this was a monumental event in British history, its immediate impact in Lower Canada (now Quebec) was limited, as slavery had been on the decline in the region for decades. The abolition marked the end of the transatlantic slave trade, though it would take until 1833 for full emancipation of enslaved people across the British Empire.

At the time, Lower Canada was largely focused on agricultural development and navigating the growing tensions between English and French-speaking residents. The abolition of slavery was a step toward broader human rights advancements in the Empire, but its relevance to Simeon's rural upbringing in Châteauguay may have been distant or indirect.

SIMEON SPOONER WAS 19 years old in 1821 when the Hudson's Bay Company (HBC) and the North West Company (NWC) merged. This merger marked the end of a fierce rivalry between the two fur-trading giants in Canada. The competition had often turned violent, with both companies vying for control of lucrative fur resources across the vast territories.

The merger created a single, dominant fur-trading entity under the HBC, with headquarters in London and trading posts extending from the Arctic to the United States border. This consolidation had a significant impact on Canada's economic and social landscape, as it led to changes in trade routes, settlements, and Indigenous partnerships. For someone like Simeon living in Châteauguay, Quebec, the merger might have had indirect effects, such as shifts in local trade goods or news of the consolidation reaching his community.

SIMEON SPOONER WAS 24 years old in 1826 when friction matches were invented by English chemist John Walker. These matches, also called "lucifers," were a groundbreaking innovation, providing a simple and reliable way to produce fire. Before this invention, people relied on more cumbersome methods like flint and steel or carrying embers from an existing fire.

The invention of matches would have eventually impacted daily life, making fire-starting much easier for households and businesses. For Simeon, living in Châteauguay, Quebec, this innovation might have taken some time to reach him, but it would have represented a step forward in convenience and safety for tasks such as lighting candles, stoves, or fireplaces.

SIMEON SPOONER WAS 35 years old during the Upper and Lower Canadian Rebellions of 1837-1838. These uprisings were fueled by political and social unrest, with reformers in both regions demanding responsible government and protesting against the entrenched power of colonial elites.

In Lower Canada (modern Quebec), the rebellion was led by the Patriotes, who sought to address grievances related to cultural and economic inequality between the French-speaking majority and the English-speaking elite. In Upper Canada (modern Ontario), William Lyon Mackenzie spearheaded the reform movement, focusing on democratic governance and land allocation issues.

Living in Châteauguay, Quebec, Simeon would have been in close proximity to the heart of the Lower Canadian rebellion. This period would have been tense and uncertain, with sporadic skirmishes and the looming presence of British military forces. The aftermath saw harsh reprisals, including executions, deportations, and a restructuring of the political system, which eventually paved the way for the union of Upper and Lower Canada in 1841.

SIMEON SPOONER WAS 46 years old in 1848 when the principles of responsible government were established in Canada. This significant political development marked the transition to a system where the executive council (or government) was accountable to the elected legislative assembly rather than the appointed governor. This change came after decades of reform movements and demands for more democratic governance following events like the 1837-1838 rebellions.

For someone like Simeon, living in a rapidly evolving society, this shift would have signaled a new era of political stability and inclusivity, allowing citizens to have a more direct influence on governance through their elected representatives. This change likely impacted his community and others in Canada East (formerly Lower Canada) by fostering greater local decision-making and aligning policies with the needs of the population.

IN 1861, SIMEON SPOONER was 59 years old, an Anglican, and a farmer residing in Storrington, Ontario. By this time, Storrington was a small but growing rural community. Farming was the backbone of the local economy, and as a farmer, Simeon would have been engaged in cultivating crops, tending livestock, and contributing to the agricultural needs of the area.

Being Anglican, Simeon likely participated in church activities, which were a central part of social and spiritual life in the community. The 1860s in Ontario were a period of increasing agricultural innovation, with farmers adopting new tools and methods. Simeon's life would have been shaped by these changes, as well as by the connections between settlers in the area, many of whom had roots in Ireland, England, and Scotland.

GENEALOGY ITINERARY:

Day 1: Arrival in Quebec

- Morning: Arrive in Montreal, Quebec. Check into your hotel and rest after your flight.

- Afternoon: Visit the Bibliothèque et Archives nationales du Québec (BAnQ) to explore genealogical records and historical documents that might provide more information about Simeon Spooner's early life.

- Evening: Enjoy a traditional Quebecois dinner at a local restaurant.

Day 2: Châteauguay, Quebec

- Morning: Travel to Châteauguay, where Simeon Spooner was born in 1802

https://www.findagrave.com/memorial/91873679/Simeon-Spooner

Visit local archives and libraries to search for birth records and other relevant documents.

- Afternoon: Explore the Châteauguay Historical Society and local churches, such as the St. Joachim Church, which might have historical records of baptisms and other church activities.

- Evening: Stay overnight in a charming bed and breakfast in Châteauguay.

Day 3: Historical Sites in Quebec

- Morning: Visit local cemeteries in Châteauguay to find more detailed records of the Spooner family.

- Afternoon: Head back to Montreal and prepare for your flight to Ontario.

- Evening: Fly to Toronto, Ontario.

Day 4: Arrival in Ontario, Canada

- Morning: Arrive in Toronto and drive to Storrington, Ontario.

- Afternoon: Check into your accommodation in Storrington. Visit the Storrington and District Museum to learn about the local history and Simeon Spooner's life as an Anglican farmer in the 1860s

https://www.findagrave.com/memorial/91873679/simeon-spooner

- EVENING: RELAX AND enjoy the scenic views of the Rideau Lakes area.

Day 5: Exploring Storrington

- Morning: Visit local churches in Storrington, such as the Anglican Church, to find baptism, marriage, and burial records.

- Afternoon: Explore the Heritage Property Index for Storrington Township to find historical sites and land records

Family of Lazarus SPOONER ALL - Genealogy.com[1]

- EVENING: ENJOY A peaceful evening by the lake.

Day 6: Kingston, Ontario

- Morning: Drive to Kingston, Ontario. Visit the Shoal Tower National Historic Site and the Kingston Association of Museums, Art Galleries & Historic Sites

Place:Storrington, Frontenac, Ontario, Canada - Genealogy[2]

The Storrington and District Museum - Times Past[3]

---

1. https://www.genealogy.com/forum/surnames/topics/spooner/668/

2. https://www.werelate.org/wiki/Place:Storrington%2C_Frontenac%2C_Ontario%2C_Canada

- AFTERNOON: EXPLORE the 1000 Islands History Museum in Gananoque to learn more about the region's history

Heritage Property INdex » Storrington Township[4]

- EVENING: RETURN TO Storrington for your final night.

Day 7: Departure

- Morning: Spend your last morning in Storrington, perhaps revisiting any sites of interest or conducting final research.

- Afternoon: Drive back to Toronto for your flight home.

- Evening: Depart from Toronto, concluding your genealogical journey.

I hope this itinerary helps you connect with Simeon Spooner's past and uncover more about his life and heritage!

---

3. http://www.storringtonmuseum.org/the_collection/times_past/

4. https://ontario.heritagepin.com/storrington-township-in-frontenac/

JANE (PATTON) SPOONER

J ANE (PATTON) SPOONER[41]

JANE SPOONER, NÉE PATTON, was born in Ireland in 1807, a time when Ireland was part of the United Kingdom and undergoing significant changes due to industrialization and political unrest. Her early life in Ireland would have been influenced by these factors, as well as by the challenges of rural life and the socio-economic conditions of the era.

By the time she emigrated to Canada, likely with her family or after her marriage to Simeon Spooner, she would have faced the challenges of settling in a new land, including adapting to the harsh Canadian climate and the demands of pioneer life.

JANE PATTON WAS 14 years old in 1821 when the Hudson's Bay Company and the North West Company merged. This merger ended a period of intense and often violent competition between the two fur trading companies in Canada. The unification brought about a significant shift in the fur trade, consolidating resources and creating a vast network of trade routes.

For someone in Ireland, this event would have been distant news, but it symbolized the expanding influence of British colonial enterprises in North America, a continent that many Irish people would later migrate to, including Jane herself. This merger played a role in shaping the economic and cultural landscape of Canada, the country she would eventually call home.

JANE PATTON WAS 30 years old in 1837 when the Upper and Lower Canadian Rebellions took place. These uprisings were significant events in Canadian history, driven by frustrations with colonial governance, lack of representation, and issues like land distribution and political corruption.

The rebellions were spearheaded by reformers seeking responsible government, with William Lyon Mackenzie leading the efforts in Upper Canada and Louis-Joseph Papineau in Lower Canada. Although the uprisings were ultimately suppressed, they brought attention to the need for political reform, eventually leading to the establishment of responsible government in the Province of Canada in the 1840s.

Living in Ireland at that time, Jane might have been focused on life closer to home. However, the rebellions and their outcomes would later influence the society she joined in Canada, where she settled as a farmer's wife in Storrington, Ontario.

JANE PATTON WAS 41 years old in 1848 when the principles of responsible government were established in Canada. This pivotal moment marked a significant shift in the governance of British North America, granting elected representatives greater power and accountability to the public rather than to colonial governors or British officials.

For settlers like Jane, who would later move to Canada, this development shaped the democratic and political landscape of the country they were joining. It ensured that local governments were more responsive to the needs of their communities, paving the way for political stability and reforms that influenced daily life in growing towns and rural areas like Storrington, Ontario.

———

IN 1861, JANE WAS 54 years old, living with her husband Simeon in Storrington, Ontario. As an Anglican and a farmer's wife, her days would have been busy with managing household duties, assisting with farm work, and participating in church and community activities. Life would have revolved around family, faith, and ensuring the farm's success in the growing settlement.

GENEALOGY ITINERARY:

Day 1: Arrival in Ireland

• Morning: Arrive in Dublin, Ireland. Check into your hotel and rest after your flight.

• Afternoon: Visit the National Library of Ireland to explore genealogical records and historical documents that might provide more information about Jane Patton's early life.

• Evening: Enjoy a traditional Irish dinner at a local pub.

Day 2: County Antrim, Ireland

• Morning: Travel to County Antrim, where many Pattons were historically located

Irish Genealogy[1]

---

1. https://irishgenealogy.ie/en/

Visit local archives and libraries to search for birth records and other relevant documents.

• Afternoon: Explore the Public Record Office of Northern Ireland (PRONI) and local churches, which might have historical records of baptisms and other church activities.

• Evening: Stay overnight in a charming bed and breakfast in County Antrim.

Day 3: Historical Sites in Ireland

• Morning: Visit local parishes in County Antrim to find more detailed records of the Patton family.

• Afternoon: Head back to Dublin and prepare for your flight to Canada.

• Evening: Fly to Toronto, Ontario.

Day 4: Arrival in Ontario, Canada

• Morning: Arrive in Toronto and drive to Storrington, Ontario.

• Afternoon: Check into your accommodation in Storrington. Visit the Storrington and District Museum to learn about the local history and Jane Spooner's life as a farmer's wife in the 1860s

Access Irish Genealogy Records[2]

• EVENING: RELAX AND enjoy the scenic views of the Rideau Lakes area.

Day 5: Exploring Storrington

---

2. https://www.gov.ie/en/service/access-irish-genealogy-records/

- Morning: Visit local churches in Storrington, such as the Anglican Church, to find baptism, marriage, and burial records.

- Afternoon: Explore the Heritage Property Index for Storrington Township to find historical sites and land records

Jane Patton Spooner (1807-1891) - Find a Grave Memorial[3]

- EVENING: ENJOY A peaceful evening by the lake.

Day 6: Kingston, Ontario

- Morning: Drive to Kingston, Ontario. Visit the Shoal Tower National Historic Site and the Kingston Association of Museums, Art Galleries & Historic Sites

Heritage Property INdex » Storrington Township[4]

Place:Storrington, Frontenac, Ontario, Canada - Genealogy[5]

- AFTERNOON: EXPLORE the 1000 Islands History Museum in Gananoque to learn more about the region's history

The Haunted Walk[6]

- Evening: Return to Storrington for your final night.

Day 7: Departure

---

3. https://www.findagrave.com/memorial/258114606/jane-spooner

4. https://ontario.heritagepin.com/storrington-township-in-frontenac/

5. https://www.werelate.org/wiki/Place:Storrington%2C_Frontenac%2C_Ontario%2C_Canada

6. https://hauntedwalk.com/

• Morning: Spend your last morning in Storrington, perhaps revisiting any sites of interest or conducting final research.

• Afternoon: Drive back to Toronto for your flight home.

• Evening: Depart from Toronto, concluding your genealogical journey.

I hope this itinerary helps you connect with Jane Spooner's past and uncover more about her life and heritage!

THOMAS SPOONER

THOMAS SPOONER[42]

Thomas Spooner was born in Upper Canada in 1839, during a period of social and economic transition in the region. The year 1839 marked the aftermath of the Upper and Lower Canada Rebellions, which had occurred in 1837-1838. These rebellions highlighted widespread dissatisfaction with the governance system, eventually leading to significant reforms, including the 1841 Act of Union that united Upper and Lower Canada into the Province of Canada.

Growing up, Thomas would have witnessed the gradual evolution of his community as settlers cleared land for farming, built roads, and established schools and churches. The agricultural economy was dominant, and families like the Spooners were deeply tied to their land and local Anglican community. By the time Thomas reached adulthood, Upper Canada had undergone significant political and social changes that would shape his life and future.

THOMAS SPOONER WAS 8 years old in 1847 when the principles of responsible government were established in the Province of Canada. This political reform marked a significant step toward democracy, ensuring that the government was accountable to elected representatives rather than colonial authorities.

As a young boy growing up in a farming family, Thomas likely wouldn't have fully understood the political changes, but their effects would have shaped his community. Local governance became more representative, and the voices of settlers in rural areas like Upper

Canada gained more influence. This period would have set the stage for the development of the region where Thomas lived and farmed.

———————————

IN 1861, THOMAS SPOONER was 22 years old, Anglican, and living in Storrington, Ontario, with his family. As part of a farming household, Thomas would have been actively involved in agricultural work, which was the primary occupation in rural Ontario at the time. The Anglican Church played a significant role in the social and spiritual life of the community, and its teachings would have influenced his upbringing and daily life.

Storrington, being a rural township, would have offered a close-knit community where families supported one another through farming activities and local events. The area was still developing infrastructure like roads and schools, and daily life would have revolved around hard work, church, and family.

MARY ANN SPOONER

ARY ANN SPOONER[43]

Mary Ann Spooner was born in Upper Canada in 1841, a time when the region was transitioning from a British colony into a more self-governing province. Families like hers lived in a predominantly rural setting, with farming being the cornerstone of their livelihood. As a young girl, Mary Ann would have grown up in a household where everyone contributed to daily tasks, from tending to the animals to helping with household chores.

By 1841, Upper Canada had just united with Lower Canada to form the Province of Canada, a major political shift. Her early childhood coincided with these changes, which would later shape the governance and development of the area where she lived.

Mary Ann grew up in a close-knit, Anglican farming community where church and family provided structure and support. Education for girls in rural areas was often limited, but she may have learned basic reading and writing skills at home or in a local school, if one was nearby.

MARY ANN SPOONER WAS 7 years old in 1848 when the principles of responsible government were established in the Province of Canada. This marked a significant shift in political power, giving elected officials more authority and reducing the dominance of appointed British governors.

At the time, Mary Ann's life would have revolved around her family's farm and local community in rural Upper Canada. News of political developments likely came through word of mouth, newspapers, or sermons at church. While these changes may not have directly impacted her daily life, they shaped the world she was growing up in, laying the groundwork for the more democratic society her family would live in over the coming decades.

IN 1851, MARY ANN SPOONER, at around 10 years old, was living in Storrington Township, Ontario, with her family. Life in rural Upper Canada at the time revolved around farming, community, and religion. Storrington was part of the agricultural heartland of Canada West, and the Spooner family would have been deeply engaged in farm work and the rhythms of the seasons.

For Mary Ann, daily life likely included helping her mother with household chores, preparing food, and caring for younger siblings. As an Anglican family, Sundays would have been devoted to church attendance and rest, reinforcing the values and traditions of the community. Storrington was a close-knit township, and social interactions were often centered around church and farming activities.

The 1850s were also a time of gradual change, as railroads were being built, towns were growing, and new immigrants continued to arrive, shaping the landscape of Upper Canada into what would later become modern Ontario.

IN 1861, MARY ANN SPOONER, now around 20 years old, was Anglican and still living in Storrington Township, Ontario. As a young adult in a rural community, her life would have likely been centered around family responsibilities, church activities, and social events within the township.

During this time, Storrington remained a predominantly agricultural area. Mary Ann might have been helping her family manage their farm or preparing for her future, possibly considering marriage or other opportunities that were common for women of her age. The Anglican Church likely played a significant role in her life, providing a spiritual foundation and a social network within the community.

The broader context of 1861 in Canada West included the ongoing debates about Confederation and the economic and cultural growth of the region. For Mary Ann, these changes may have seemed distant, as her daily life was likely focused on the immediate needs and routines of rural life.

ANDREW SPOONER

A NDREW SPOONER[44]

Andrew Spooner, Mary Ann's twin, was born in Upper Canada (now Ontario) in 1841. Growing up as part of a farming family in rural Storrington Township, his childhood would have been marked by hard work, close family ties, and participation in the Anglican Church, which likely served as a cornerstone of their community life.

Historical Context:

Andrew's early years were shaped by a developing Canada. In 1841, the same year he was born, the Act of Union united Upper and Lower Canada into the Province of Canada. This merger aimed to bring political stability and encourage economic growth. As Andrew grew, he would have witnessed or heard about the social and political changes leading up to the establishment of responsible government in 1848.

By 1861, Andrew, now 20 years old, was likely working alongside his family on their farm. Farming would have been a demanding occupation, requiring physical labor and knowledge of seasonal cycles. Life in Storrington would have revolved around agriculture, church gatherings, and local events. Like his twin sister Mary Ann, Andrew was Anglican and living in Storrington at this time.

FANY SPOONER

FANY SPOONER[45]

Fany Spooner was born in Canada West (modern-day Ontario) in 1845, during a time of significant growth and development in the region. As the youngest of the Spooner siblings, her early life would have been spent on the family farm in Storrington Township. Growing up in a rural community, she likely helped with household and farm duties from a young age, learning the skills and responsibilities typical for girls of her time.

Historical Context:

Childhood Events: Fany was born the same year that significant Irish immigration began in Canada due to the Great Famine. The influx of Irish immigrants shaped many communities in Canada West, contributing to its cultural and economic diversity.

Social Environment: By the time she was 3, the sewing machine had been patented, a development that would eventually revolutionize domestic life.

FAMILY LIFE:

As part of an Anglican family, church attendance and religious education would have been integral to her upbringing. By 1861, at the age of 16, Fany would have been transitioning into adulthood, helping more extensively on the farm and possibly preparing for a future that could include marriage and starting her own household. Like her siblings, she lived with her family in Storrington, where agriculture and community events shaped their daily lives.

RICHARD HUGES

R ICHARD HUGES[46]

Richard Hughes was born in Canada West (now Ontario) in 1843, a time when the region was undergoing rapid development and societal change. His early life would have been shaped by the rural and agricultural lifestyle common in the area, as well as by the cultural and economic influences of the mid-19th century.

Historical Context:

Infancy and Childhood: Richard was born just two years after the Act of Union (1841), which united Upper and Lower Canada into the Province of Canada. This political change aimed to address economic and governance issues in the colonies.

Local Impact: The mid-1840s saw a significant wave of Irish immigration due to the Great Famine, which contributed to population growth and diversified communities in Canada West.

LIFE IN CANADA WEST:

By the time he was 7, the Principles of Responsible Government (1850) had been established, marking a shift towards self-governance in the Province of Canada. During his teenage years, Richard would have witnessed the economic and social changes brought about by increasing industrialization and infrastructure improvements, such as the expansion of railroads.

In 1861, Richard was 18 years old and likely contributing to his family's livelihood, whether through farming, trade, or other work common in rural Ontario. His Anglican upbringing would have been central to his family and community life, emphasizing religious education and moral values.

GENEALOGY ITINERARY:

DAY 1: ARRIVAL IN ONTARIO

• Destination: Kingston, Ontario

• Activities:

• Check-in: Settle into your accommodation.

• Orientation: Visit the local tourism office for maps and information.

Day 2: Storrington Township

• Destination: Storrington, Ontario

• Activities:

• Visit Local Archives: Start at the Frontenac County Archives to search for local records.

• Explore Storrington: Walk around the township to get a feel for the area where Richard lived in 1861.

• Anglican Church: Visit the local Anglican church to inquire about parish records.

Day 3: Kingston Research Day

• Destination: Kingston, Ontario

- Activities:

- Library and Archives Canada: Spend the day researching birth, marriage, and death records.

- Kingston Frontenac Public Library: Check their genealogy section for local histories and records.

Day 4: Land and Property Records

- Destination: Kingston, Ontario

- Activities:

- Ontario Land Registry Office: Search for any land transactions involving Richard Huges.

- Local Historical Society: Visit the Kingston Historical Society for additional resources and insights.

Day 5: Church Records and Cemeteries

- Destination: Storrington, Ontario

- Activities:

- Parish Registers: Continue your search for baptism, marriage, and burial records at local Anglican churches.

- Cemetery Visit: Explore local cemeteries for any gravesites of Richard Huges or his family members.

Day 6: Surrounding Areas

- Destination: Nearby Towns and Villages

- Activities:

- Explore Nearby Archives: Visit archives in neighboring towns for additional records.

- Historical Sites: Check out any historical sites or museums that might provide context about the era Richard lived in.

Day 7: Wrap-Up and Departure

- Destination: Kingston, Ontario

- Activities:

- Review Findings: Spend the morning reviewing and organizing your research.

- Departure: Head back home with your newfound knowledge and records.

Tips for Your Trip

- Prepare in Advance: Contact archives and libraries ahead of time to confirm hours and any requirements for accessing records.

- Bring Supplies: Take notebooks, a camera, and a portable scanner to document your findings.

- Stay Flexible: Be prepared to adjust your itinerary based on what you discover along the way.

Enjoy your journey into the past and the adventure of uncovering Richard Huges' story!

JAMES SPOONER

JAMES SPOONER[47]

James Spooner was born in 1833 in Upper Canada, a colony that was still relatively young and focused on agriculture and settlement. His formative years were shaped by a rapidly evolving society with a growing population and the development of local infrastructure.

Historical Context:

1830s in Upper Canada: The colony was undergoing political tensions as reform movements gained momentum, eventually culminating in the Upper Canada Rebellion of 1837 when James was four years old.

Economic Life: Agriculture dominated the economy, and families were self-reliant, with farming as the primary livelihood.

Community Life: Settlements were expanding, and communities were centered around churches and schools, with religion playing a significant role in daily life.

CHILDHOOD AND EARLY Life:

James grew up during a time of transition from colonial dependence to a push for responsible government. As a young boy, he likely helped with farm work and other family duties, learning skills essential for rural living. Education would have been limited to local schools, but literacy was becoming more common among families who valued it.

By the time he reached adulthood, Upper Canada had become Canada West in 1841, following the union of Upper and Lower Canada into the Province of Canada. These political changes likely shaped his awareness of identity and governance as he moved into his adult years.

WHEN JAMES SPOONER was 6 years old, in 1839, photography became publicly available with the invention of the daguerreotype process by Louis Daguerre in France. This innovation revolutionized how people captured and preserved memories.

Impact on the Time:

First Images: The daguerreotype created sharp, single images on polished silver-plated copper, making portraits possible for the first time.

Cultural Change: Photography offered families and individuals a way to document their lives visually, a privilege previously limited to painted portraits for the wealthy.

Arrival in Canada: It didn't take long for daguerreotypists to bring the technology to North America, including Canada, where traveling photographers began offering portraits in towns and villages.

ALTHOUGH PHOTOGRAPHY was still in its infancy, its potential to preserve moments and record history marked the beginning of a cultural shift. James, living in rural Upper Canada, would likely have first encountered photography later in life as the technology spread beyond cities.

WHEN JAMES SPOONER was 13 years old, in 1846, the sewing machine was patented by Elias Howe in the United States. This invention revolutionized textile manufacturing and household sewing by significantly increasing efficiency and reducing manual labor.

Impact at the Time:

Textile Industry Boom: Factories began adopting sewing machines to mass-produce garments, which led to the growth of ready-made clothing industries.

Economic Opportunities: The sewing machine created jobs, particularly for women, in both factories and homes, as it became a tool for piecework.

Household Use: While initially expensive, sewing machines became more accessible in the 1850s, transforming household labor for families like James's.

LIVING IN UPPER CANADA, James may not have directly encountered a sewing machine during its early years, but its impact on the economy and daily life would gradually ripple through his community.

IN 1861, JAMES SPOONER, at 28 years old, was a Presbyterian blacksmith residing in Storrington, Ontario. As a blacksmith, James played a vital role in his community, crafting and repairing essential tools, agricultural equipment, horseshoes, and household items. His work would have been physically demanding but highly respected, as blacksmiths were indispensable to rural economies.

Life in Storrington in 1861:

Community and Religion: As a Presbyterian, James would have been part of a close-knit religious community, attending church services and participating in social gatherings centered around his faith.

Agricultural Economy: Storrington was primarily a farming region, and James's skills as a blacksmith would have been essential for maintaining the tools and equipment that local farmers relied on.

Daily Challenges: He likely faced challenges like long work hours, dependence on raw materials such as iron and coal, and adapting to new agricultural innovations.

Canadian Milestones: In 1861, Canada West (now Ontario) was moving toward Confederation (1867), and societal changes such as advancements in transportation, industry, and education were beginning to influence rural areas like Storrington.

JAMES'S WORK AS A BLACKSMITH made him a cornerstone of his community, ensuring that both agricultural and domestic life could function smoothly.

GENEALOGY ITINERARY:

DAY 1: ARRIVAL IN ONTARIO

- Destination: Kingston, Ontario

- Activities:

- Check-in: Settle into your accommodation.

- Orientation: Visit the local tourism office for maps and information.

Day 2: Storrington Township

- Destination: Storrington, Ontario

- Activities:

- Visit Local Archives: Start at the Frontenac County Archives to search for local records.

- Explore Storrington: Walk around the township to get a feel for the area where James lived in 1861.

- Presbyterian Church: Visit the local Presbyterian church to inquire about parish records.

Day 3: Kingston Research Day

- Destination: Kingston, Ontario

- Activities:

- Library and Archives Canada: Spend the day researching birth, marriage, and death records.

- Kingston Frontenac Public Library: Check their genealogy section for local histories and records.

Day 4: Land and Property Records

- Destination: Kingston, Ontario

- Activities:

- Ontario Land Registry Office: Search for any land transactions involving James Spooner.

- Local Historical Society: Visit the Kingston Historical Society for additional resources and insights.

Day 5: Church Records and Cemeteries

• Destination: Storrington, Ontario

• Activities:

• Parish Registers: Continue your search for baptism, marriage, and burial records at local Presbyterian churches.

• Cemetery Visit: Explore local cemeteries for any gravesites of James Spooner or his family members.

Day 6: Surrounding Areas

• Destination: Nearby Towns and Villages

• Activities:

• Explore Nearby Archives: Visit archives in neighboring towns for additional records.

• Historical Sites: Check out any historical sites or museums that might provide context about the era James lived in.

Day 7: Wrap-Up and Departure

• Destination: Kingston, Ontario

• Activities:

• Review Findings: Spend the morning reviewing and organizing your research.

• Departure: Head back home with your newfound knowledge and records.

Enjoy your journey into the past and the adventure of uncovering James Spooner's story!

MARGARET (CURRAN) SPOONER

M ARGARET (CURRAN) SPOONER[48]

Margaret Curran, later Margaret Spooner, was born on January 9, 1842, in Portland Township, Upper Canada. Growing up in the early 19th century in a rural township, Margaret would have experienced a life centered around family, farming, and community.

Life in Portland Township in the 1840s:

Family and Work: As a child in a farming community, Margaret likely helped with household chores and farm duties from a young age. This included tasks like cooking, sewing, tending to livestock, and helping with crops.

Education: Education opportunities for girls in rural Upper Canada were limited but growing. Margaret might have attended a local one-room schoolhouse, learning basic reading, writing, and arithmetic.

Religion: Depending on her family's denomination, religion would have played a significant role in her upbringing, with Sunday church services being a central part of life.

Community: Life in Portland Township revolved around cooperation and mutual support among neighbors, with social events such as barn raisings, quilting bees, and church gatherings.

HISTORICAL CONTEXT:

Era of Change: Margaret was born shortly after Upper and Lower Canada united into the Province of Canada (1841). This was a time of political reform and growing settlement in rural Ontario.

Advances in Daily Life: Although technology like sewing machines and steam-powered equipment was being introduced, life in Portland Township would still have been largely traditional and self-reliant during Margaret's childhood.

BY THE TIME SHE MARRIED James Spooner, she would have been well-prepared for the challenges of supporting a household and contributing to their rural community in Storrington, Ontario.

MARGARET CURRAN WAS 5 years old in 1847 when the Principles of Responsible Government were established in the Province of Canada. This political reform was a milestone in Canadian history, giving the elected Assembly more power and accountability to the people rather than the Crown.

Impact on Margaret's Early Life:

Family Discussions: While Margaret was too young to fully grasp political changes, her family and community would have likely discussed the shift toward greater local control and self-governance. These changes influenced the social and political environment in which she grew up.

Shaping Society: The establishment of responsible government marked the start of a more democratic and participatory political culture, which would affect the opportunities and freedoms available to future generations, including Margaret's own children.

MARGARET CURRAN AND James Spooner's Wedding in 1858

A wedding in 1858 Frontenac, Ontario, would have reflected the modesty, practicality, and traditions of rural 19th-century Canada, influenced by their Presbyterian faith and the customs of their time.

THE CEREMONY:

Location: Likely held in a church or private home, as many rural areas had small congregations that gathered in modest venues. The ceremony would have been officiated by a Presbyterian minister.

Length: The service would have been solemn and brief, focusing on scripture readings, vows, and prayers. Presbyterian weddings avoided extravagant rituals, keeping the focus on faith and commitment.

Guests: Close family and friends, often limited in number due to travel difficulties and smaller social circles in rural communities.

THE RECEPTION:

Likely hosted in the family home or a local community hall.

Food would have been home-cooked, featuring seasonal dishes such as roasted meats, stews, root vegetables, fresh-baked bread, pies, and preserves.

Entertainment might include fiddle music, dancing, and traditional songs. In a modest rural setting, celebrations would focus on family togetherness.

WHAT THEY MIGHT HAVE Worn:

Margaret's Wedding Attire:

Dress: A practical yet elegant dress made of heavy fabric like silk, wool, or taffeta, in colors such as brown, grey, or blue—white dresses were rare for rural brides at the time. Her dress would likely be repurposed for future formal occasions.

Style: A fitted bodice with a high neckline and long sleeves, paired with a full skirt supported by petticoats or a crinoline hoop, reflecting mid-19th-century fashion.

Accessories:

A simple bonnet or veil, possibly trimmed with lace.

Gloves for formality.

Modest jewelry, such as a brooch or a family heirloom.

SHOES: STURDY LEATHER shoes, possibly dyed to match her dress.

JAMES' WEDDING ATTIRE:

Suit: A tailored wool suit in dark colors such as black, navy, or charcoal.

Shirt: A crisp white or light-colored shirt with a high collar.

Cravat or Tie: A modest cravat or necktie, tied simply.

Accessories:

A waistcoat, likely in a subtle pattern or color to complement his suit.

Pocket watch, a sign of practicality and status.

***

SHOES: POLISHED LEATHER boots suitable for both the wedding and everyday wear.

***

WEATHER CONSIDERATIONS in November:

With a November wedding, warmth would have been essential. Margaret may have worn a shawl, cloak, or cape for the journey, and James likely donned a warm overcoat.

***

SYMBOLISM:

Their attire and ceremony would have emphasized practicality, faith, and respectability—key values in their Presbyterian and rural community. The wedding would reflect their commitment to each other and their readiness to build a life together in their shared faith.

***

BY 1861, AT 18 YEARS old, Margaret Curran was a young wife and likely adjusting to her life with James Spooner in Storrington, Ontario. As a Presbyterian, her life would have revolved around her faith, household duties, and community.

Daily Life in 1861:

Home Life: As a farmer's wife, Margaret would have been responsible for cooking, cleaning, and maintaining the household. She may also have helped with farm tasks like gardening, preserving food, or tending to livestock.

Faith: Attending church services and observing Sabbath practices were central to her routine. Presbyterianism emphasized simplicity, devotion, and a close-knit community.

Clothing: Margaret would have worn practical yet modest dresses, typically made from wool or cotton, with high necklines and long sleeves. An apron was common for daily tasks.

Social Role: Her position as a young wife would have required learning the customs and expectations of her new household and balancing her role as a homemaker with her place in the local community.

———

MARGARET AND JAMES, as newlyweds, likely worked together to establish a stable and prosperous life. Their faith and family connections would have provided support as they began their journey as a couple in rural Ontario.

GENEALOGY ITINERARY:

———

DAY 1: ARRIVAL IN ONTARIO

- Destination: Kingston, Ontario

- Activities:

- Check-in: Settle into your accommodation.

- Orientation: Visit the local tourism office for maps and information.

Day 2: Portland Township

• Destination: Portland Township, Ontario

• Activities:

• Visit Local Archives: Start at the Rideau Lakes Public Library to search for birth records and local histories.

• Explore Portland Township: Walk around the area to get a feel for where Margaret was born in 1842.

Day 3: Storrington Township

• Destination: Storrington, Ontario

• Activities:

• Visit Local Archives: Head to the Frontenac County Archives to search for records from the 1860s.

• Explore Storrington: Visit the township to understand the environment where Margaret lived as a farmer's wife in 1861.

• Presbyterian Church: Visit the local Presbyterian church to inquire about parish records.

Day 4: Kingston Research Day

• Destination: Kingston, Ontario

• Activities:

• Library and Archives Canada: Spend the day researching birth, marriage, and death records.

• Kingston Frontenac Public Library: Check their genealogy section for local histories and records.

Day 5: Land and Property Records

• Destination: Kingston, Ontario

• Activities:

• Ontario Land Registry Office: Search for any land transactions involving Margaret Spooner or her family.

• Local Historical Society: Visit the Kingston Historical Society for additional resources and insights.

Day 6: Church Records and Cemeteries

• Destination: Storrington, Ontario

• Activities:

• Parish Registers: Continue your search for baptism, marriage, and burial records at local Presbyterian churches.

• Cemetery Visit: Explore local cemeteries for any gravesites of Margaret Spooner or her family members.

Day 7: Surrounding Areas

• Destination: Nearby Towns and Villages

• Activities:

• Explore Nearby Archives: Visit archives in neighboring towns for additional records.

• Historical Sites: Check out any historical sites or museums that might provide context about the era Margaret lived in.

Day 8: Wrap-Up and Departure

- Destination: Kingston, Ontario

- Activities:

- Review Findings: Spend the morning reviewing and organizing your research.

- Departure: Head back home with your newfound knowledge and records.

ENJOY YOUR JOURNEY into the past and the adventure of uncovering Margaret Spooner's story!

DAVID McGOWAN

DAVID McGOWAN[49]

David McGowan, born in Upper Canada in 1831, would have grown up in a rapidly changing society as the area transitioned into modern Canada. His early years were shaped by rural life and the social, political, and economic developments of the time.

Key Events During His Youth:

1. 1837-1838 Rebellions: At six years old, David would have heard of the Upper and Lower Canada Rebellions, which pushed for more democratic governance.

---

2. UNION OF THE CANADAS (1841): When he was ten, Upper and Lower Canada united as the Province of Canada, marking a pivotal political shift.

---

3. PRINCIPLES OF RESPONSIBLE Government (1848): At 17, he witnessed a step toward democracy as Canada West and East gained more self-governance.

RURAL LIFE IN UPPER Canada:

Daily Life: Growing up in a farming community, David likely learned skills such as crop cultivation, livestock care, and carpentry. Rural families were self-reliant, making most of what they needed.

Education: Access to formal education was limited, often depending on the establishment of local schools. If he attended, he learned basic literacy and arithmetic.

Clothing: Boys and men wore durable, homespun wool or linen clothing. A shirt, trousers, and a waistcoat were typical for everyday wear, with sturdy boots or shoes.

CULTURAL IDENTITY:

David's identity would have been shaped by his family's background, whether Irish, Scottish, English, or otherwise. Religion likely played a central role in his upbringing, influencing his values and community connections.

IN 1861, DAVID MCGOWAN was 30 years old, Catholic, and living in Storrington, Ontario. His Catholic faith likely played a significant role in his daily life, providing community support, moral guidance, and a connection to his heritage.

Life as a Catholic in Storrington (1861):

1. Religious Practices:

Regular attendance at Mass and participation in sacraments would have been central to his routine.

Catholic churches served as community hubs, fostering connections with other Irish or French Catholic families in the area.

2. OCCUPATION AND DAILY Life:

As a resident of Storrington, he may have been involved in farming or manual labor, which were common occupations in rural Ontario.

Rural Catholics often worked hard to support their families and contribute to the growing local economy.

---

3. COMMUNITY CHALLENGES:

Catholics in predominantly Protestant regions sometimes faced discrimination or social tension, though Ontario's multicultural rural areas often encouraged cooperation.

Social and Cultural Life:

Catholic Festivities: Feast days and church events provided opportunities for fellowship and celebrations.

Clothing: David would have worn practical attire suited for his work—linen or wool shirts, trousers with suspenders, and sturdy boots. On Sundays or for church gatherings, he might have donned a jacket and hat to present his best self.

HIS FAITH AND POSITION in the rural landscape would have defined much of his identity and role in the community.

GENEALOGY ITINERARY:

Day 1: Arrival in Kingston, Ontario

- Morning: Arrive in Kingston, Ontario. Check into a local hotel.

- Afternoon: Visit the Kingston Frontenac Public Library to explore historical records and archives. Look for any documents related to David McGowan's birth in 1831.

- Evening: Enjoy a leisurely dinner at a local restaurant and rest for the next day's activities.

Day 2: Exploring Kingston and Surroundings

- Morning: Visit the Archives of Ontario in Kingston. Search for birth, marriage, and death records from the early 19th century

Search: Births, Marriages and Deaths recorded in Canada - Library and Archives Canada[1]

• AFTERNOON: TAKE A guided tour of Fort Henry, a significant historical site from the era when David McGowan was born.

• Evening: Stroll along the Kingston waterfront and enjoy the scenic views.

Day 3: Journey to Storrington Township

• Morning: Drive to Storrington Township, located in Frontenac County.

• Afternoon: Visit the Storrington Township Historical Society. Explore local archives and historical records, including the 1861 census

https://www.familysearch.org/search/catalog/313462

• EVENING: STAY OVERNIGHT in a nearby bed and breakfast or a local inn.

Day 4: Discovering Storrington's History

• Morning: Visit St. Patrick's Catholic Church in Storrington. This church may have records of David McGowan's religious activities and community involvement.

• Afternoon: Explore the local cemeteries to find gravestones and memorials that might provide more information about the McGowan family.

• Evening: Enjoy a quiet evening reflecting on the day's discoveries.

Day 5: Research and Relaxation

---

1. https://www.bac-lac.gc.ca/eng/discover/vital-statistics-births-marriages-deaths/births-marriages-deaths-recorded/Pages/search.aspx

- Morning: Return to Kingston for further research at the Kingston Frontenac Public Library or the Archives of Ontario.

- Afternoon: Visit the Murney Tower Museum to learn more about the historical context of the area during David McGowan's lifetime.

- Evening: Relax and enjoy a farewell dinner in Kingston.

Day 6: Departure

- Morning: Check out of your hotel and prepare for your journey home.

- Afternoon: If time permits, take a final walk through Kingston's historic downtown area.

This itinerary should provide a comprehensive exploration of David McGowan's life and the historical context of Upper Canada and Storrington Township. Enjoy your genealogical journey!

ADAM SMITH

A DAM SMITH[50]

Adam Smith, born in Ireland in 1825, came into the world during a time of significant social and political change. Ireland was marked by agricultural dependence, increasing population pressure, and a volatile relationship with Britain.

Life in Ireland in 1825:

1. Agricultural Economy:

The economy heavily relied on tenant farming, with most families renting small plots from landlords to grow potatoes, oats, and other staples.

The potato, a nutritious and reliable crop, was the primary food source, especially for rural families like Adam's.

---

2. POLITICAL LANDSCAPE:

The Catholic Emancipation Movement was gaining momentum under Daniel O'Connell, advocating for Catholic rights in a Protestant-dominated system.

Tensions over land ownership, poverty, and governance shaped daily life.

---

3. SOCIAL LIFE:

Rural communities were tight-knit, with life revolving around the local parish and traditional Irish customs, music, and storytelling.

Education was limited, with hedge schools providing informal instruction in some areas.

Childhood Challenges:

Adam's early years would have been defined by the stark divide between the wealthy landowners and impoverished tenant farmers. Hunger, disease, and the struggle for rights were persistent challenges. His family's religious affiliation (Protestant or Catholic) would have greatly influenced his opportunities and experiences in a deeply divided society.

WHEN ADAM SMITH WAS 1 year old in 1826, matches, as we recognize them today, were invented. These were "friction matches," created by John Walker, an English chemist. This innovation marked a shift in daily life by making fire-starting quicker, safer, and more convenient compared to flint and steel or other traditional methods.

For Adam's family in rural Ireland, this new technology likely wouldn't have been accessible right away due to cost or limited availability. They would have continued using older methods for lighting fires, as matches became commonplace only later in the century. The invention symbolized progress during a time when life for most Irish families remained rooted in traditional practices and tools.

WHEN ADAM SMITH WAS 12 years old in 1837, the Upper and Lower Canadian Rebellions took place. These uprisings were driven by frustrations with colonial governance and a push for greater democratic rights.

Though Adam was in Ireland at the time, news of the rebellions likely reached Europe through newspapers and letters. The unrest in British North America may have resonated with Irish communities, as Ireland was also grappling with issues of land reform, self-determination, and dissatisfaction with British rule. For Adam and his family, these events might have highlighted the growing tensions within the British Empire, which would have seemed particularly relevant as Irish people faced their own struggles under British authority.

BY 1861, ADAM SMITH was a 36-year-old Presbyterian farmer living in Storrington, Ontario, with his wife. As a farmer, his life would have revolved around the agricultural calendar, growing crops like wheat, oats, and barley, and raising livestock to support his family and contribute to the local economy.

Living in Storrington meant Adam was part of a rural community that valued hard work, faith, and neighborly support. Presbyterianism likely played a significant role in his life, influencing his moral values and weekly routines through church attendance and community involvement. Farming required resilience and resourcefulness, as he would have faced challenges like unpredictable weather, limited technology, and market fluctuations.

The 1861 census reflects a period when settlers like Adam were helping establish Storrington as an agricultural hub, contributing to the development of the province during a time of political and economic transformation in Canada West.

GENEALOGY ITINERARY:

Day 1: Arrival in Dublin, Ireland

• Morning: Arrive in Dublin, Ireland. Check into a local hotel.

• Afternoon: Visit the National Library of Ireland to explore birth records and other historical documents from 1825.

• Evening: Enjoy a traditional Irish dinner and rest for the next day's activities.

Day 2: Exploring Dublin's Archives

• Morning: Visit the General Register Office to search for Adam Smith's birth records and any other relevant documents.

• Afternoon: Explore the Irish Emigration Museum to understand the context of Irish emigration during the 19th century.

• Evening: Take a stroll through Dublin's historic streets and enjoy the local culture.

Day 3: Journey to Storrington, Ontario

• Morning: Fly from Dublin to Kingston, Ontario.

• Afternoon: Drive to Storrington Township, located in Frontenac County.

• Evening: Check into a local bed and breakfast or inn in Storrington.

Day 4: Discovering Storrington's History

• Morning: Visit the Storrington Township Historical Society to explore local archives and historical records, including the 1861 census

https://www.familysearch.org/search/catalog/313462

• AFTERNOON: VISIT St. Andrew's Presbyterian Church in Storrington. This church may have records of Adam Smith's religious activities and community involvement.

• Evening: Explore the local area and enjoy a quiet evening.

Day 5: Research and Exploration

• Morning: Visit the Kingston Frontenac Public Library to search for additional historical records and documents related to Adam Smith's life in Ontario.

• Afternoon: Explore the Frontenac County Museum to learn more about the history of the region during the 19th century.

• Evening: Relax and enjoy a dinner in Kingston.

Day 6: Exploring Local Cemeteries

• Morning: Visit local cemeteries in Storrington to find gravestones and memorials that might provide more information about Adam Smith and his family.

• Afternoon: Continue exploring the area or return to the Archives of Ontario in Kingston for further research.

• Evening: Reflect on your discoveries and enjoy a farewell dinner.

Day 7: Departure

• Morning: Check out of your hotel and prepare for your journey home.

• Afternoon: If time permits, take a final walk through Kingston's historic downtown area.

This itinerary should provide a comprehensive exploration of Adam Smith's life and the historical context of Ireland and Storrington Township. Enjoy your genealogical journey!

[1] https://www.wikitree.com/wiki/Shannon-7157#Ancestors

[2] https://www.wikitree.com/wiki/Shannon-7158#Ancestors

[3] https://www.wikitree.com/wiki/Unknown-703943

[4] https://www.wikitree.com/wiki/Connell-4507#Ancestors

[5] https://www.wikitree.com/wiki/Shainon-1#Ancestors

[6] https://www.wikitree.com/wiki/Waldron-3610#Ancestors

[7] https://www.wikitree.com/wiki/Unknown-703974#Ancestors

[8] https://www.wikitree.com/wiki/Waldron-3614#Ancestors

[9] https://www.wikitree.com/wiki/Waldron-3615#Ancestors

[10] https://www.wikitree.com/wiki/Waldron-3617#Ancestors

[11] https://www.wikitree.com/wiki/Waldron-3616#Ancestors[1]

[12] https://www.wikitree.com/wiki/Watters-1823#Ancestors

[13] https://www.wikitree.com/wiki/Unknown-704261#Ancestors

[14] https://www.wikitree.com/wiki/Watters-1824#Ancestors

[15] https://www.wikitree.com/wiki/Watters-1825#Ancestors

[16] https://www.wikitree.com/wiki/Watters-1826#Ancestors

[17] https://www.wikitree.com/wiki/Hobbs-10862#Ancestors

[18] https://www.wikitree.com/wiki/Neely-3168#Ancestors

[19] https://www.wikitree.com/wiki/Unknown-704907#Ancestors

[20] https://www.wikitree.com/wiki/Neely-3169#Ancestors

[21] https://www.wikitree.com/wiki/Neely-3170#Ancestors

1. https://www.wikitree.com/wiki/Waldron-3616#Ancenstors

[22] https://www.wikitree.com/wiki/Neely-3171#Ancestors

[23] https://www.wikitree.com/wiki/Neely-3172#Ancestors

[24] https://www.wikitree.com/wiki/Neely-3173#Ancestors

[25] https://www.wikitree.com/wiki/Chambers-15094#Ancestors

[26] https://www.wikitree.com/wiki/Unknown-704953#Ancestors

[27] https://www.wikitree.com/wiki/Chambers-15095#Ancestors

[28] https://www.wikitree.com/wiki/Chambers-15096#Ancestors

[29] https://www.wikitree.com/wiki/Chambers-15097#Ancestors

[30] https://www.wikitree.com/wiki/Chambers-15098#Ancestors

[31] https://www.wikitree.com/wiki/Nobbs-537#Ancestors

[32] https://www.wikitree.com/wiki/Unknown-705013#Ancestors

[33] https://www.wikitree.com/wiki/Nobbs-538#Ancestors

[34] https://www.wikitree.com/wiki/Nobbs-539#Ancestors

[35] https://www.wikitree.com/wiki/Nobbs-540#Ancestors

[36] https://www.wikitree.com/wiki/Howes-3553#Ancestors

[37] https://www.wikitree.com/wiki/Unknown-705078#Ancestors

[38] https://www.wikitree.com/wiki/Shannon-7164#Ancestors

[39] https://www.wikitree.com/wiki/Shannon-7165#Ancestors

[40] https://www.wikitree.com/wiki/Spooner-2754#Ancestors

[41] https://www.wikitree.com/wiki/Patton-9827#Ancestors

[42] https://www.wikitree.com/wiki/Spooner-2755#Ancestors

[43] https://www.wikitree.com/wiki/Spooner-2756#Ancestors

[44] https://www.wikitree.com/wiki/Spooner-2757#Ancestors

[45] https://www.wikitree.com/wiki/Spooner-2758#Ancestors

[46] https://www.wikitree.com/wiki/Huges-99#Ancestors

[47] https://www.wikitree.com/wiki/Spooner-2759#Ancestors

[48] https://www.wikitree.com/wiki/Curran-3749#Ancestors

[49] https://www.wikitree.com/wiki/McGowan-4592#Ancestors

[50] https://www.wikitree.com/wiki/Smith-357754#Ancestors

Don't miss out!

Visit the website below and you can sign up to receive emails whenever Angeline Gallant publishes a new book. There's no charge and no obligation.

https://books2read.com/r/B-A-QGSI-EJKLF

BOOKS 2 READ

Connecting independent readers to independent writers.

Also by Angeline Gallant

A Dragon's Diary
Dreaming of Dragons

Blood and Spirit Saga
The Rising Wind
Fate's Promise

Calling Her Heart
Whisper of the Heart
Calling Her Heart Boxed Set Volumes 1-4
Calling Her Heart Volumes 1 & 2: A Small Town Romance
Collection
No Turning Back
Calling Her Heart volumes 3 & 4
Forsake Me Not
Hear My Cry

FORGET ME NOT

Victoria, Ontario's Babies 1894 - 1895

Guardian of the Heart
Fallen Petals

Keeper Of Secrets
A Lady's Secret

Kingston's Love Chronicles
Springtime Promises

Midnight's Awakening
Heart of the Storm
Walking Through The Storm
Walking Through The Storm
Fighting the Storm
Call Me Cursed
Heart of the Storm

Secrets of the Underworld
Deklan's Dragons

Tell My Story Collection

Tell My Story: Germany 1851
Tell My Story: England 1852
Whispers From The Garrison Church

The Dervock Legacy
Echoes of Dervock

The Grave Whisperer
German Prisoners of War in Canada
Cataraqui United Church Cemetery
Whispers of Kingston
Wedding Bells in Kingston, Ontario, Canada 1923
St. Paul's Anglican Churchyard A-B
St. Paul's Anglican Churchyard C-D
St. Paul's Anglican Churchyard E - F
St. Paul's Anglican Churchyard G - H
St. Paul's Anglican Churchyard J - N
St. Paul's Anglican Churchyard O - R
St. Paul's Anglican Churchyard S - T
St. Paul's Anglican Churchyard, Kingston, Ontario T - Z
Small Graveyards & Burial Grounds: Kingston, Ontario, Canada
Cataraqui United Church Cemetery 1
Cataraqui United Church Cemetery 2
Cataraqui United Church Cemetary 3
Cataraqui United Church Cemetery 4
Cataraqui United Church Cemetery 5
Beth Israel Cemetery
Cataraqui United Church Cemetery 6
Beneath the Surface: Echoes from Beth Israel Cemetery
Grave Tales: Discovering the Lives of Beth Israel

Whispers Beneath St. Paul's
Unveiled

The Timeless Veil
Eternal Devotion

The Wolf Whisperer Series
The Cry of the Wolf
Journey of the Heart
Captured Heart
Fate's Legacy
Mohawk Valley
Cry of a Warrior
Wolf Whisperer volumes 1 & 2
Endless White
The Wolf Whisperer Volumes 1-4
The Wolf Whisperer volumes 1 & 2

Timeless
The Time Keeper's Sanctuary

Timeless Echoes
Timeless Roots
Echoes of Storrington

Timeless Whispers of Dervock Saga
Secrets of Dervock

Standalone
Winds of Change vol 1-3

Watch for more at https://www.goodreads.com/author/show/
19703964.Angeline_Gallant.

About the Author

Angeline Gallant traces her roots through generations of Old Stock Canadian heritage, her passion for genealogy as deep and enduring as the forests and fields her ancestors once walked. With a reverence for history and an eye for detail, she weaves stories from the fragments of lives left behind in letters, records, and weathered headstones.

An avid reader and devoted writer, Angeline brings the past to life with a curiosity for heraldry and a deep love for the landscapes that shaped her family's story. Each name and date she uncovers feels less like history and more like coming home, a familiar echo in the vast tapestry of time. For her, these stories are not forgotten—they live, breathing in the quiet spaces of memory and tradition, a testament to lives once lived, now eternal in the pages of her books.

Read more at https://www.goodreads.com/author/show/19703964.Angeline_Gallant.

About the Publisher

At Crest & Quill Press, we bring history to life, one story at a time. Specializing in genealogy, heraldry, and historical fiction and nonfiction, we are passionate about uncovering the past and celebrating the stories that shape our world today.

From tales of noble lineages and family legacies to immersive historical sagas, our books are crafted for readers who crave a deeper connection to their roots and a richer understanding of history. Whether you're exploring the crests of your ancestors or diving into vivid narratives of bygone eras, Crest & Quill delivers stories that resonate and endure.

With a dedication to authenticity, storytelling, and the preservation of history, Crest & Quill Press is your gateway to the past—and a celebration of its impact on the present and future.